STILL LIFE
WITH A BRIDLE

Other Books by Zbigniew Herbert
from The Ecco Press

Report from the Besieged City
and Other Poems
Translated by John and Bogdana Carpenter

Selected Poems
Translated by Czeslaw Milosz
and Peter Dale Scott

STILL LIFE
WITH A BRIDLE

ESSAYS AND APOCRYPHAS

❑

Zbigniew Herbert

*Translated by
John and Bogdana Carpenter*

THE ECCO PRESS
New York

The Ecco Press
26 West 17th Street
New York, NY 10011
Published simultaneously in Canada by
Penguin Books Canada Ltd., Ontario
Printed in the United States of America
Designed by Debby Jay
First Edition

Grateful acknowledgment is made to the editors of the following publications in which these essays first appeared: "Epilogue," "The Hell of Insects," "Home," "Letter," "Long Gerrit," *"Perpetuum Mobile,"* and "Spinoza's Bed," in *Artful Dodge;* "The Price of Art" in *The Antioch Review;* and "Delta" in *Salmagundi.*

Library of Congress Cataloging-in-Publication Data

Herbert, Zbigniew.
[Martwa Natura z Wędzidłem. English]
Still life with a bridle: essays and apocryphas / by Zbigniew
Herbert: translated [from the Polish] by John and Bogdana
Carpenter.—1st ed.
p.   cm.
Translation of: Martwa Natura z Wędzidłem.
1. Art, Dutch. 2. Art, Modern—17th–18th centuries—Netherlands.
I. Title.
N6946.H4713   1991   709'.492'09032—dc20   91-15707   CIP
ISBN 0–88001–306–0

The text of this book is set in New Baskerville

This translation was made possible in part through a grant from The Wheatland Foundation, New York.

Contents

❏

STILL LIFE
WITH A BRIDLE

ESSAYS

DELTA

❏

The visible world would be more perfect if seas and
continents had a regular shape.
                    —MALEBRANCHE
                    Méditations chrétiennes.

"Imensi Tremor Oceanii"
                    —Inscription on a sarcophagus
                    of Michiele de Ruyter.
                    Amsterdam, Nieuwe Kerk.

JUST after crossing the Belgian-Dutch border, suddenly and
without reason or reflection I decided to change my original
plan. Instead of the classical road to the north I chose the
road to the west, in the direction of the sea. I wanted to get
to know Zeeland, even if superficially; I had never been there.
All I knew was that I would not experience great artistic revelations.

Until now my travels through Holland had always followed
the movement of a pendulum along the coast. That is, to
speak graphically, from Bosch's "Prodigal Son" in Rotterdam
to "The Night Guard" in Amsterdam's Royal Museum, a tra-
jectory typical for someone who devours paintings, books, and
monuments, leaving all the rest to those who, like the Biblical
Martha, care only for earthly things.

3

At the same time I realized my limitations, because clearly the ideal traveler knows how to enter into contact with nature, with people and their history as well as their art. Only familiarity with these three overlapping elements can be the starting point of knowledge about a country. This time I allowed myself the luxury of leaving behind "essential and important" things in order to compare monuments, books, and paintings with the real sky, the real sea, and real land.

So we are driving through an enormous plain, a civilized steppe, the road as smooth as an airport runway amid endless meadows similar to the flat green paradise in the polyptych of the van Eyck brothers in Ghent. Though nothing extraordinary happens, though I am prepared because I have read about it a hundred times, changes still take place in my sensory apparatus that are difficult to describe yet at the same time very concrete. My eyes of a city dweller, unused to the expansive landscape, fearfully and uncertainly check the faraway horizon as if learning to fly above an unattainable surface. It is similar to a huge overflow rather than a mainland, which in my experience is always associated with an accumulation of elevations, mountains, rising cities that break the line of the horizon. This is why I was in a state of constant alarm during my journeys in Greece and Italy, a never-ending need to reach a broader "birdlike" perspective that would allow me to take in the whole image, or at least a great part of it. This is why I climbed the steep slope of Delphi, strewn with marble, to see the spot of the mortal duel of Apollo with the beast. This is why I tried to climb Olympus in the illusory hope of embracing the entire Valley of Thessaly from sea to sea (to my misfortune, the gods had an important meeting in the clouds just at that moment, so I saw nothing). I also patiently polished winding steps in the towers of Italian city halls and churches. But my efforts were rewarded only with something that could be called a "torso of a landscape"—splendid, of course splendid fragments. Later they became pale and I arranged them in my memory like postcards, these deceitful images with false colors and false light, untouched by emotion.

Here in Holland, I had a feeling the smallest hill would be enough to take in the entire country: all its rivers, meadows, canals, its red cities, like a huge map that one can bring closer or move farther from the eyes. It was not at all a feeling accessible to lovers of beauty, or purely aesthetic. It was like a particle of the omnipotence that is reserved for the highest beings: to embrace the limitless expanse with its wealth of detail, herbs, people, waters, trees, houses, all that is contained only in God's eye—the enormous magnitude of the world and the heart of things.

Thus we drive through a plain that puts up no resistance, as if the laws of gravity were suddenly suspended. We move with the motion of a sphere on a smooth surface. We are overwhelmed by a powerful sensual feeling, blessed monotony, sleepiness of the eyes, dulled hearing, and the retreat of touch because nothing happens around us to cause anxiety or exaltation. Only later, much later, do we discover the fascinating richness of the great plain.

A STOP in Veere. It is reasonable to begin the sightseeing of a country not from its capitals or spots marked with "three stars" in a guide but precisely from a godforsaken province abandoned and orphaned by history. A matter-of-fact and laconic Baedeker from 1911 I never part with has devoted twelve cool lines to Veere ("manche Erinerungen aus seiner Blutezeit"), while my precious Guide Michelin flies on the wings of touristlike *poésie de circonstance:* "Une lumière douce, une atmosphère ouatée et comme assoupie donnent à Veere l'allure d'une ville de légende . . . Ses rues calmes laissent le visiteur sous un charme mélancolique."

Indeed Veere, once famous, populous, and rich, is now a degraded, make-believe city; it is deprived of its own life like a moon reflecting the life and light of others. Only in the summer as a "porte de plaisance" is it filled with a crowd of merry nomads; afterward it goes underground and leads the secret existence of plants. In the fall it gives the impression of a drawing from which the artist has removed people in order to put city walls, buildings, and facades into relief. Streets and squares are empty, shutters closed. No one answers a ringing at the gates.

It looks as if the town was touched by an epidemic but the whole drama carefully concealed, victims removed behind the deceitful decorations of an idyll. A huge number of shops with antiques. At the day's end their windows look like cemeteries in the gentle light of dusk, huge still lifes.

A cane with a silver handle has a romance with a fan.

The square with the city hall is lit with amber light; a pretty building, with sculpted details but strong at the same time, sits squatly on the ground, proof of old splendor. A number of sculptures in niches on the facade: portraits of councillors, mayors, and benefactors of local history.

During my night wanderings I come upon a powerful building, thickset and smooth—a sculpture of God without a face. It emerges from the night similar to a rock growing from the ocean; not a single ray of light reaches this place. A dark mass of primordial matter against the background of night's blackness.

AN attack of alienation, but a gentle one that touches most people transported into a foreign place. A sense of the otherness of the world, a conviction that nothing happening around takes me into account, that I am superfluous, rejected, and even ridiculous with my grotesque intention to see the old church tower.

6

In a state of alienation the eyes react quickly to objects and banal events that do not exist for the practical eye. I am surprised by the color of mailboxes, tramways, different shapes of copper doorknobs, knockers on doors, stairs always winding in a dangerous way, wooden shutters whose surface is crossed by two straight diagonal lines, a big "X" and the four fields of these big "X"s alternately filled with black and white, or white and red paint.

I know I waste too much time listening to a painted street organ huge as a gypsy's wagon, and also on the steps of the post office where I stand staring at a green vehicle coming out of Aaron and Moses streets. It stirs up clouds of dust by setting brushes in its chassis into a whirling motion, which might not be the ideal way of cleaning a city but is a serious warning that dust will never find peace here.

Petty events, small street-fragments of reality.

It happens that my wanderings without any plan bring unexpected profit. For a long time Binnenhof, or its interior courtyard, has been my favorite architectural complex in the center of The Hague. Surrounded by a pond, almost quiet in the late afternoon, as my master Fromentin says, "It is an exceptional place, very solitary and not deprived of melancholy, especially when one comes at this time of day, when one is a foreigner and the joyful years no longer keep a man company. Imagine a great pool encircled by stiff embankments and black palaces. On the right a tree-lined, empty promenade, on the left Binnenhof emerging out of the water with its brick facade, its slate-covered roof and grim expression, its physiognomy from another century or rather from all centuries, full of tragic memories, concealing an atmosphere characteristic of places on which history has left its traces . . . Exact but colorless reflections fall on the sheet of sleeping water with that somewhat deadly immobility of recollections which distant life leaves in extinguishing memory."

The romantic Mr. Fromentin spins out meditations about lofty things, history, beauty, fame. I, however, with all the force of my spirit cling to the brick. Never yet has this angular object awakened in me such fascination and fever to find out more about it.

Dusk is falling, the last acrid, Egyptian yellows go out, cinnabar becomes gray and fragile, the last fireworks of the day grow dark. All of a sudden there is an unexpected pause, a short-lasting interval in the darkness as if somebody in a hurry opened the door from a light room to a dark room. It happens as I sit on a bench several yards from the back wall of the Ridderzall, the Knights' Hall. For the first time I have the impression that the Gothic wall is like a fabric: perpendicular, taut, without any decorations, tightly woven with thick yarn and a narrow, stringy, pithy warp. The scale of colors is contained between ochre and umber with caprate added. The tint of the bricks is not uniform. From time to time a fawn-brown appears like a half-baked roll or the color of a fresh, crushed cherry, then again a mysterious violet covered with glaze. Instructed by the Knights' Hall, I start to appreciate the old, warm, close-to-the-earth brick.

During all my daily pacing of the street pavements and museum parquet floors, a tantalizing thought never leaves me: that my wanderings will be sterile if I do not manage to reach the interior, the inside of Holland untouched by the human hand and identical with what was looked at by my collective hero, the Dutch bourgeois of the seventeenth century. Only then could we exist in the same frame, against an eternal landscape.

The advertisements of the tourist agencies are banal and without imagination, the schedules of bus offices deprived of taste like the dinners of railway-station restaurants.

I wait thus for pure chance; and chance appears under the seductive name Valley of the River Lek and River List.

The valley is like a bowl, and so green, black-green and violet-green, that everything becomes steeped in this thick damp color. Only the River Isel retains its ashy color, like a flag of sovereignty before it drowns in the immensity of other waters.

On the left side of the road leading to Rotterdam, a herd of motionless windmills. This is the only view I take with me on the journey like a talisman.

Thus I am in Holland, the kingdom of things, great principality of objects. In Dutch, *shoen* means beautiful and at the same time clean, as if neatness was raised to the dignity of a virtue. Every day from early morning a psalm of washing, bleaching, sweeping, carpet beating, and polishing hovers over the whole land. What has disappeared from the surface of the earth (but not from memory), what the ramparts of attics have protected is found in five regional museums with fairy-tale names: Ede, de Lutte, Apelddoom, Lievelde, Marssum, Helmonie. One can find there hundred-year-old coffee grinders, kerosene lamps, machines for drying marshes and irrigating fields, shoes for weddings and every day, instructions for polishing diamonds and forging harpoons, models of grocery stores, tailor shops, pastry shops, recipes for baking and holiday cakes, a drawing representing a huge shark on an ocean beach, and three ominous meteors.

I ask myself: why precisely in this country are a great-grandmother's bonnets, a cradle, a great-grandfather's frock coat made from Scottish wool, and a spinning wheel preserved with special care, an almost religious attention? The attachment to things was so great that pictures and portraits of objects were commissioned as if to confirm their existence and prolong their lives.

In numerous Renaissance and baroque pamphlets the Dutch appeared invariably as money-grubbers, penny-pinchers obsessed with the desire to possess. But true wealth was rare. It

9

was limited almost exclusively to the regents, those who traditionally occupied the highest state and provincial offices. The Calvinist church did not advocate general poverty, it was only against ostentatiousness in clothes, delights of the table, and magnificent carriages. Luckily a number of ways existed to alleviate a conscience tormented by an excess of worldly possessions—for instance, founding poorhouses for children and old people—which led to a social system without equal in the world.

Money could be reason for pride. In his funereal epitaph the respectable merchant Isaak le Maire passes over his virtues and good deeds but mentions (it might seem not very elevated for a voice from beyond the grave) a fortune he leaves behind of 150,000 guldens.

WE are now driving north but cannot see the ocean; it is concealed by a dike several yards high and the color of sand. Below, at a distance of many miles, an incredible movement: trucks, bulldozers, people who look as if they were putting foundations under the Tower of Babel. In fact it is polder, retrieved from the sea bottom and dried, a new piece of land on which houses will stand in a year, with a lush meadow and majestic cows.

HOLLAND is a young country—on a geological scale of course (postdiluvian). In fact it was a delta, a powerful mixture of the elements of earth and water: the Schelde, the Rhine, and the Weser. The old maps clearly show how the sea pitilessly encroached upon the land with powerful thrusts in the north as well as in the western provinces of Zeeland and Holland.

In a letter to Germaine de Staël Bejamin Constant wrote, "This brave nation lives with all that it possesses on a volcano, the lava of which is water." This has not a word of exaggeration. It could be said that throughout its history Holland lost more people as a result of floods than during all its wars. Even taking into consideration the tendency of old chroniclers to exaggerate, the balance sheet is grim. The huge north bay of Zuidersee was the result of a natural disaster that took fifty thousand human lives. In the eighteenth century, thirty-five floods were registered. One could prolong almost endlessly the list of these cemeteries without gravestones. Water attacked also the great cities of Haarlem, Amsterdam, and Leyden; when in 1421 the ring closed around Dordrechtuw, one could see from its tower only a desert of water, without a single living soul.

The systematic struggle with flood disasters started at the turn of the sixteenth century. It was the work of excellent artisans and engineers, not to mention self-taught geniuses. Jan Leeghwater undoubtedly belonged to their number, and thanks to his works he achieved the somewhat exaggerated nickname of the Dutch Leonardo da Vinci. The range of his interests was indeed Renaissance-like: he built a city hall in Rijp, he sculpted and did some painting, his works in metal, wood, and ivory enjoyed great popularity. He constructed ordinary as well as musical clocks and a huge number of machines to dry the soil.

Leeghwater thought that the addition of witchcraft and mystery could not harm science but on the contrary might help it. He organized shows to which he invited an elite audience. In France in the presence of Prince Maurice he demonstrated a machine in the shape of a bell: he let himself be drowned in the machine, and under water wrote a psalm taken from the Bible, fortified his body with a few pears, then appeared to the court whole, healthy, and bursting with energy.

AFTER several days I grew accustomed to the thought that I would not see the views painted by the Dutch masters of the "Golden Age." In Italy it is enough to lean out the train window to see a fragment of Bellini flash in front of your eyes, or the sky of Umbria as it was registered ages ago. In Holland I found instead the largest collection of landscapes that were contained in frames. The Flamand Patenier, who painted in the sixteenth century, shone like a guiding star: a master of spaces built from perpendicular screens and brown, green, and blue perspectives. Then came others; constellations and hierarchies kept changing. The fabulous mannerists Coninxlo and Sebery, simple-hearted Avercamp, Cuyp, Potter, the painter of the apotheosis of artiodactylus, Hobbema, and Momper, to mention only a few of my favorite landscape painters.

The knowledge I received in school—it is well known that this is a bundle of correct facts as well as dogmatic idiocies—left me with the conviction that the greatest landscape painter was Jacob Ruysdael. "Toward the end of the seventeenth century at a time when painters specialized in specific thematic genres, this landscape painter with an unusual personality, knowledge, and insatiable curiosity recorded in his works in a matchless manner the indissoluble union of water, land, and sky characteristic of the Dutch landscape. No one else was able to show in such a moving way the mutual harmony of atmospheric values and the shape of clouds."

This tirade of a well-known scholar, more inspired than lucid, raises Ruysdael to the rank of cherubim. In the words of the illustrious though unrestrained art historian, the painter becomes an archangel. I was faithful to him for so many years, and continued to revere his epic canvases, calm, painted from a perspective of the dunes where one can see spreading meadows, stripes of white linen on them, and on the horizon the respectable city of Haarlem with the powerful Church of Saint Bawon, wings of windmills glimmering in the sun. Above it all the huge sky (its relation to the land one to four). I always worshiped Ruysdael; but as a guide through old, provincial Holland, I chose Jan van Goyen.

I would still like to say why my feelings for Ruysdael cooled. Well, it happened when spirit began to enter his canvases and everything became "soulful," every leaf, every broken branch, drop of water. Nature was sharing our own anxieties and sufferings, transitoriness and death. For me nature that lacks compassion is the most beautiful: a cold world in another world.

THREE large, low-lying rivers with their tributaries, thousands of brooks and streams, a huge drainage of water called the Haarlem Sea, all this created favorable conditions for communication. Highways shaded by trees were often built next to the canals, from Delft to The Hague, from Leyden to Amsterdam; they met with general approval and pride. William Temple, the English ambassador at The Hague for a long time, maintained that the road from Scheveningen to The Hague (barely a few kilometers) could be ranked with "the work of the Romans," which was an exaggeration.

The situation changed with the seasons. The public stagecoach, introduced in the middle of the seventeenth century, had four wheels but no springs, causing an unbearable jolting of travelers; the whole vehicle dragged behind it clouds of dust that covered everything. The Estates General imposed a normalized set of wheels on vehicles, which was reasonable; they also strengthened the highway police, especially in forested terrain. Brigands caught red-handed were punished on the spot and without trial. Huygens, a statesman, humanist, poet, and sensitive man, did not like to waste his time even when traveling—riding along the bank of the Rhine, he counted the imposing number of fifty gallows on a road less than twenty kilometers long. This was his contribution to the statistics of verdicts that were carried out.

The car creaks, squeaks, rolls with difficulty on a hummock of land—the light is now like honey—one more curve, on the left a cluster of birches strongly bent toward the canal's water heavy with browns and shadowy greens, the smell of slime and rotting tree trunks. On the right something that with a great dose of fantasy might be called a farm: a house with plaster peeling from its walls, the roof a hundred-year-old map of storms, a tall brick chimney like a turret repelling the last assault. What country is it? Whose domain? What is the name of the ruler?

Setting out with my favorite landscape painter, Jan van Goyen, I was not sure whether we would ride a highway on land or a road of the imagination. Goyen painted a number of so-called "Village Lanes," and we have tried to describe one of these. The outline is simple, beginning at the base of the painting: a narrow canal, a sandy sprawling road, a shed or something that once upon a time was a house and today is a picturesque ruin, a few scrawny trees, and a goat, the heraldic animal of poverty.

All this elicits many questions. Where did the enthusiasts for this subject matter come from in prosperous Holland? Were there any such alleys of poverty in the country? (My guide, Jan van Goyen, completely convinces me with the magic of his art.) Where does the true Troy and Eliot's Wasteland exist?

A road through a village, a ferry floating down the river, a hut among dunes, clusters of trees and haystacks, travelers waiting for a ride—these are the typical subjects of Goyen's paintings. Canvases with no anecdote, loosely composed, flimsy and slim, with a weak pulse and nervous outline, they quickly leave their imprint on the memory. The eye assimilates them without any resistance, and they remain on the retina for a long time. When I first saw Goyen's painting I felt I had waited a long time for just this painter, that he filled a gap in the museum of my imagination I had sensed for a long time. It was accompanied by an irrational conviction that I knew him well and forever. From where did Goyen take the themes of his canvases? Sometimes it can be determined without difficulty on the basis of the fragments of the architecture he represents.

In the large painting in the Museum of Art History in Vienna we easily recognize the churches and towers of Dordrecht on great, gray water cut by waves shaped like half-moons and regular as ornaments. But in the beautiful painting in Munich's Pinakotheka, "View of Leyden," the painter moved the Church of Saint Pankras outside the city, placing it on a peninsula surrounded by water on both sides. The old, intricate Gothic church towers above a group of fishermen, shepherds, and cows on the far shore of an imaginary landscape. Often the topography of his works is unclear: somewhere beyond the dune, on the shore of some river, at the turn of a road, on a certain evening. . . . It was said the master had the cheapest elementary props in his atelier you can imagine: clay, brick, lime, pieces of plaster, sand, straw. From these leftovers, rejected by the world, he created new worlds.

In his middle period Goyen painted a number of excellent monochromatic works dominated by bistre, sepia, and heavy green. The Dutch did not invent the method of painting with a single color but endowed it with grace and naturalness, because monochromatism is an accurate epitome of visible reality, a rendering of sheen and atmosphere (a blue-gray glow a moment before a storm, the light of summer afternoons heavy with lazy gold).

This great painter managed his talent very poorly. He was an appreciated, prolific artist, but the fact that he sold his paintings for the beggarly price of five to twenty-five guldens barred his chances of a serious career. No one with self-respect, unless constrained to do so, would sell his canvases for a price only slightly higher than the cost of materials.

He started to learn his profession very early, as a ten-year-old boy: he changed his masters five times, finally entering the atelier of Esaias van de Velde, not much older than himself and creator of excellent landscapes that seem washed by rain. Goyen did not settle down in a single place. He led a rather nomadic life, traveled to Germany and England, and returned with portfolios of sketches. His drawings are quick, impressionistic, and without many details, executed as if with a single stroke of the pencil not lifted from the paper. He always preferred a narrow palette of complementary colors to a painting constructed from many contrasts; in this sense he remained a monochromatic painter to the end.

When he was almost forty-five he settled down in The Hague, which did not in the least mean financial stability. So he had tried everything.

He did not lack ideas. He traded the paintings of his colleagues, organized auctions, speculated on houses and land and also the wretched tulips.

The result of these commercial acrobatics was a double bankruptcy and death in debts. His malicious contemporaries maintained that his only favorable transaction was matrimonial; he married his daughter to a shrewd and canny innkeeper, the painter Jan Steen.

What emerges from fog and rain, what is reflected in a drop of water? Jan van Goyen's "Landscape of Objects" is in the Dahlem Museum, a painting so small it can be covered by the hand. But it is neither a notation, a sketch, nor a trial version for a larger work; it is a full-blooded painting, self-contained, with a composition as simple as a chord. From the grayness of sky and earth emerges a clump of osiers whose fingerlike leaves are painted with a juicy dark green. From time to time among the thickets, a small yellow accent. The picture does not hang from a wall. This shred of the world was placed in a glass case, to make one bow over it.

OFTEN after my vacations I listened to conversations in which the light of faraway countries was praised. But what really is the light for which artists in the past would leave their native

16

towns, found artists' communities, profess a solar cult, and pass into history as the school from N? What is the light of Holland, so luminous for me in the paintings but absent in immediate surroundings? I decided once to devote a whole day to meteorological studies. In the morning the weather was nice but the sun seemed suspended in an opaque, viscous liquid similar to a soft light bulb, without a trace of a *l'azzurro*. The clouds appeared and quickly disappeared. Exactly at one-thirty in the afternoon it suddenly cooled off, and in half an hour torrential, heavy-grained, dark-blue rain began. It struck with fury against the ground and seemed to be returning to the sky to fall with greater implacability. It lasted about an hour. Exactly at seven in the evening I left for Scheveningen to pursue my studies further. The rain had already stopped. Piles of clouds all over the west. The resort, the cabins, the casino now dazzlingly white were covered with a coating of violet. A moment before eight everything changed: a staggering festival began, of water vapor, forms, colors, metamorphoses difficult to describe because even the evening sun sent out frivolous pinks and farcical gold.

The spectacle finished. The sky was clear. The wind stopped. Faraway lights went on and off, and all of a sudden without warning, without a breeze or anticipation, a huge cloud the color of ash appeared, a cloud in the shape of a god torn apart.

THE PRICE
OF ART

❏

Was macht die Kunst?
Die Kunst geht nach Brot.
Dass muss sie nicht, dass soll sie nicht.
—LESSING,
Emilia Galotti

A LARGE room, rather dark despite a high vaulted window on the left. Lazy daylight seeps through thick glass panes framed in lead.

Where a painter is seated, wooden easels have been placed perpendicular to the window. He wears a beret, an old, thick jacket, puffed pantaloons, and heavy, shapeless boots. He rests his right leg against the lower crossbar of the easel. His hand, with a brush, approaches the surface of the painting.

One can easily imagine his patient, irregular swinging movement: bending forward—placing the paint; leaning backward—checking the effect. A piece of paper is nailed to the upper frame of the painting: a sketch of the work being painted.

At the rear, elevated above the rest of the atelier (it is entered by steps), an apprentice grinds pigments against a darkening wall.

18

Is this how art is born? In a dark interior amid dust, cobwebs, and an indescribable disorder of objects with no grace or beauty? Even the painter's accessories—messy sketchbooks, jars, brushes, sheets of paper, a plaster cast of a head, a wooden mannequin—are degraded to the role of kitchen utensils.

There is no trace of mystery, magic, or rapture in this painting. It requires a great and devious imagination, like that of a certain art historian, to see a Faustian atmosphere here. There is no one behind the painter's back. With a small change of props, a maker of tables or a master of the needle could be working in this room.

All the subtle tastes of the aesthetes, all their fantasies must be disappointed and retreat from the thick physicalness of the work. The painter's matter is heavy, rough-hewn, and massive.

Such is the "Painter in His Workshop" by Adriaen van Ostade (1610–1685): oil on an oak board, with the dimensions 38 by 35.5 centimeters.

SEVERAL years after throwing off their foreign yoke the small Netherlands, with a population of barely two million, became a colonial empire, a flourishing, powerful country and political organism strong enough to defy powers like France, England, and Spain. In the Europe of the seventeenth century, torn by religious wars, it was an unusual, universally admired asylum of freedom, tolerance, and prosperity.

A large number of accounts by travelers who visited Holland during its "golden age" have been preserved. The young bourgeois republic intrigued visitors with the uniqueness of its lifestyle and peculiar political system, the inhabitants' antlike industriousness and inventiveness, as well as their healthy, concrete, down-to-earth attitude toward life.

William Temple, the English ambassador at The Hague and meticulous observer of the Dutch scene, noted: "Men live together like Citizens of the World, associated by the common ties of Humanity, and by the bonds of Peace, Under the impartial protection of indifferent Laws." The envoy of His Royal Highness idealized the country of his mission, which is not strange because he moved in the highest social spheres. Numerous pamphlets and lampoons of the period show that the Dutch were envied and fiercely disliked by their neighbors, who compared them to parasites feeding on human blood. Cardinal Richelieu flung abuse at them: "Bloodsuckers, starving lice." It was written that they were "merchants of butter who milk cows in the trough of the ocean, and live in forests they have sown themselves, or in swamps changed into gardens." Who could fail to notice in this sentence an unintended note of admiration?

There are also less subjective observations that touch on our subject, and, what is more important, are not seasoned with bile. Peter Mundy, who visited Amsterdam in 1640, was surprised by the passion of the Dutch for painting. Pictures could be found not only in the homes of rich bourgeois but also in various shops and taverns, even in artisans' workshops, streets, and squares. Another traveler, John Evelyn, saw a huge number of paintings at the annual fair in Rotterdam, while in other countries these were luxury objects only the rich could afford. The very fact of exhibiting them among stalls, clucking chickens, mooing cattle, junk, vegetables, fish, farm products, and household objects must have seemed very peculiar, and was difficult for an average visitor to understand.

Trying to explain this phenomenon, Evelyn let himself be carried away by fantasy when he claimed that even ordinary peasants spent two or three thousand pounds on paintings (a huge sum, equivalent to an acre of a garden or almost three acres of meadow), and that they did it from purely mercenary motives because after a certain time they sold their "collections" with a considerable profit. The English traveler was wrong. Paintings were indeed objects of speculation, but they were not the best investment of capital. It was much more profitable to lend money at interest, or, for instance, buy shares of stock.

One thing is certain: painting in Holland was omnipresent. It seems that the artists tried to augment the visible world of their small country and to multiply reality by the thousands, tens of thousands of canvases on which they recorded seashores, floodwaters, dunes, canals, distant vast horizons, and the views of cities.

The luxuriant development of Dutch painting in the seventeenth century is not associated with the name of any powerful protector, eminent person, or institution who spread a coat of patronage over the painter. When we speak of a "golden period" in the history of culture, we have a custom of always trying to find a Pericles, a Maecenas, or the Medicis.

In Holland it was different. The Princes of Orange do not seem to have noticed their native art, Rembrandt, Vermeer, van Goyen, and so many others. They preferred the representative Baroque painting of the Flamands or Italians. When Amalia van Solms, widow of Prince Frederick Henry, decided to beautify her suburban villa her choice fell precisely on a Flamand, Rubens's pupil Jacob Jordaens, a painter of sensual, large, and fat works. Lucrative orders from the court were thus out of the question. The gentry, small in number and deprived of political influence, had no ambition to support the art of their country or even to mold fashion and taste. Finally the church, traditionally a powerful protector of artists in all other countries, closed to them the doors of its temples, which displayed dignified, austere, Calvinist nakedness.

The question comes to mind: what was the material situation of the Dutch painters, and to what should we ascribe their enormous productivity? It could not have been only an idealistic love for beauty. Our answer will be complex and unfortunately not unequivocal. We are doomed to fragmentary, incomplete data, barely translatable into contemporary language.

MEMBERS of the Fraternity of Saint Luke—a proud name, which might also designate evangelical poverty—were treated as artisans, and without exception came from the lower social classes. Sons of millers, petty merchants and manufacturers, innkeepers, tailors, dyers, such was their social status and no other. And their works? They were certainly objects of aesthetic delight, but they were also creations subject to the laws of the market, the implacable laws of supply and demand.

"Each thing that is an object of exchange must be comparable to other things. This is the purpose of money, which has become an intermediary," writes Aristotle. Therefore our search must necessarily meander among boring numbers, and we will attempt to gather the spilled pebbles into a hopefully sensible whole.

It is difficult to determine the costs of supporting an "average" family (terrible term of the statisticians) of Dutch artisans in the period we are describing. We do not know the retail prices of many necessities, only wholesale prices. But we know that the cost of living almost tripled between the end of the sixteenth century and the middle of the seventeenth century. Currency lost its value. Earnings increased, but not in proportion to inflation. As usual the estates and the capital of the wealthy swelled, but the margin of indigence and even poverty was considerable.

What are we to make of a situation as fluid as life itself? What subtle surveying instruments could be used to seize the economic phenomena in all their complexity but also in a concrete place and time? On the basis of available sources one could say that in a given year a house in Amsterdam cost so much, but this is very little to go on. Sociologists, and especially their strange mutation "sociologists of art," are prodigal with florins and guldens to dazzle the reader and bestow the splendor of science, almost mathematics, on their poor knowledge.

Let us therefore use the approach that seems most sensible: to determine (when source materials make it possible) the payments and earnings in seventeenth-century Holland. We accept as a monetary unit the gulden, worth more or less as much as the florin, which was also used as currency. Other legal tender existed, but it is safer not to venture into that thicket.

Different attempts have been made with limited success to establish the relation of the gulden to contemporary currencies. The comparison with gold, a seemingly reliable measure, also turned out to be problematic; in relation to this precious metal the gulden constantly lost value. One should therefore take into account the complicated quotations of the stock exchange. One serious researcher wrote that in Rembrandt's time the gulden had a purchasing power twenty times greater than the contemporary gulden. This might be true, but years have passed since the publication of his dissertation, and the meaning of the statement, taken from the air, has evaporated back into the air.

We are dealing with a beast difficult to describe—it is better to realize this right away. Worn-out coins, talents, cistertians, ducats, Rhine thalers, are like old demons where the same eternal potentiality of good and evil is lurking, a force pushing toward crime and deeds of mercy, passion concentrated in a small piece of metal that is similar to the passion of love or a call leading to the peaks of a human career, but also under the ax of the executioner.

We can find a measure for wealth with Paul Zumthor, who presents us with the tax registers from Amsterdam in 1630. These show that about 1,500 estates were valued at 25,000 to

55,000 florins. Considerably larger estates existed, such as that of Lopez Suasso, a Portuguese who settled in Holland and lent 2 million guldens to Prince William III for his English expedition.

Physical laborers and artisans employed in manufacturing were poorly remunerated. The fate of weavers at the beginning of the century is particularly worthy of pity; in Leyden alone, twenty thousand of these unfortunate people, who received a pittance for a twelve-hour day of work, were cooped up in various hovels. Numerous revolts and disturbances improved their situation, so that by the middle of the century they earned seven guldens a week. The wages of a fisherman on a herring boat were five to six guldens a week; qualified workers such as ship carpenters and masons in large cities earned ten guldens a week.

We know nothing of the mass of ordinary people, the poor, the noisy, the ones who drank heavily or hunted constantly for any earnings. Old dictionaries transmit the names of their "professions": unlicensed traders, day laborers, peddlers. One can believe they revealed an animal resilience and determination in the craft of life, that despite everything they kept their heads above water.

THE prices of paintings and the peculiar mechanisms of the market where works of art were thrown are well known, thanks to published materials from the abundant Dutch archives.

The rich harvest of talents, the hundreds of ateliers in nearly every town of the Republic created a huge supply of paintings that exceeded the demand by far. Painters worked under the overwhelming pressure of a growing number of competitors. Art criticism did not exist. The enlightened spheres did not impose any definite taste—this was democratic but often resulted in an outstanding painter finding himself in a material situation worse than that of a less gifted colleague.

Speculation in works of art was highly developed, governed by rules totally different from aesthetic considerations.

In a recently published book J. M. Montias has checked fifty-two inventories from the years 1617–1672, preserved in the archives of Delft. He estimated the average price of a painting was 16.6 guldens (7.2 guldens for an unsigned painting). The industrious calculation is worth our attention, for it contains a valuable piece of general information. Let us try to be disloyal to statistical "truth" in favor of what is singular, full-blooded, and not comparable: the concrete price paid for concrete paintings. Here we discover an amazing range and diversity.

What determined the market price of a painting? The name of the artist and the renown of the atelier, but to an even greater extent, the subject matter. There is no reason to be indignant. The represented world or a story about people has always satisfied the need for knowledge inherent in our nature, and admiration for successful imitation is something very normal despite the prophets of sterile purity.

Both the public and seventeenth-century Dutch writers about art, such as Karel van Mander and Samuel van Hoogstraten (painters themselves), placed the so-called *historien* at the top of the genres. These were figurative compositions. A hero, a crowd, a dramatic event taken from the Bible or mythology enjoyed unabated popularity and fetched high prices. This judgment is constant, originating in antiquity (*vide* Pliny); it continued with theoreticians of Renaissance art all the way to the nineteenth century. Historical painting meant the towering peak of art.

A French traveler noted with surprise that 600 guldens were asked for a painting by Vermeer that represented only one person. It is like a distant echo of medieval standards, when the artist depicting the interior of a church was paid according to the number of columns he painted.

A Dutchman ordering market scenes from his favorite

painter requested that they have an ever-larger number of slabs of meat, more and more fish and vegetables. O the insatiable, never satisfied hunger for reality!

In theory landscapes, genre scenes, and still lifes were valued much lower than historical painting. So why does seventeenth-century Dutch art have such an abundance, even more a predominance, of works belonging to these "lower" genres? Because strong competition requires specialization; such is the law of the market. Every grocery merchant knows that for the good of his firm he must stock a special brand of tea or a particularly aromatic brand of tobacco that attracts buyers.

The same happened in art. The struggle for survival forced the painter to remain faithful to a chosen genre. Because of this a potential buyer would retain him in his eye and memory; it was universally known that Willem van de Velde, for example, was synonymous with the "Maritime Firm," and Pieter de Hooch, with the "Firm of Bourgeois Interiors." If one lovely day a portrait painter reached the conclusion that he had had enough of the fat, bloated faces of councillors and decided from then on to paint flowers—which are so much more graceful—he took an enormous risk on his shoulders. For he would lose his present clients and enter the domain of other painters who for years had specialized in bouquets of tulips, narcissuses, and roses.

AMONG so many masterpieces in the Uffizi Gallery it is easy to overlook a small painting from the brush of Frans van Mieris, "The Family Concert." It is a scene from the life of elegant Dutch society, known for its fervent passion for music. The instruments have just gone silent, and the admirers of Polyhymnia refresh themselves with wine. Against the background of a rich interior only six persons are presented, as that Frenchman who looked at Vermeer would say. Despite this the Prince of Tuscany, Cosimo III, paid a sum for the painting that was stunning by Dutch standards—2,500 guldens, 900 guldens more than the merchants who ordered Rembrandt's "Night Watch" took from their pockets.

What was the range of prices of Dutch paintings in the seventeenth century? This is a problem that cannot be reduced to a clear, comprehensible formula, or summed up in a single pale "average."

In the complicated mechanism of the trade of works of art, not only rational factors but also unpredictable chance played a role—for instance the material situation of the artist at a given moment, and the good but often bad will of the buyer, who only waited for the best moment to enter into possession of paintings and pay as little as possible.

During the period of his fame Rembrandt set hard conditions and often received as much as he asked. But others, recognized today as masters, had to be satisfied with a payment so pitiful it is difficult to understand how they avoided going under, even with the greatest industriousness.

IN 1657 a well-known antique and art dealer, Johannes Renialme, died in Amsterdam. As usual in such cases, work began immediately on a detailed inventory of his estate. In addition to property, jewelry, and curios, it included more than four hundred paintings. And what paintings: Holbein, Titian, Claude Lorraine, the most eminent Dutch masters. Next to each item a realistic market price was given, the price that could be received *hic et nunc* according to the opinion of competent painters and professional appraisers if the inheritance was to be realized. In Dutch archives many inventories are preserved that are priceless, trustworthy documents for researchers.

Rembrandt's painting "Christ and the Adulteress" was appraised highest, at the respectable sum of 1,500 guldens. This seems completely understandable because of the artist's rank and the elevated subject, belonging to those *historien* so much praised by art theoreticians. But despite the theoreticians a typical genre scene came right after Rembrandt, namely Gerard Dou's "Kitchen Maid," highly appraised at six hundred guldens. Dou was a sought-after, constantly fashionable painter. Warm, somewhat sweetish colors, a masterly play of light, immaculate, precise drawing (anecdotes were told how he spent the whole day painting brooms and brushes, each bristle separately), these won him admirers beyond Holland's frontiers as well. But other genre painters, not at all worse, were treated harshly. At the very bottom of the inventory of Johannes Renialme's estate came Brouwer, in our estimate an excellent painter, whose canvas was scandalously appraised at barely six guldens.

We can only guess at the impact of this huge range of prices on the psychology of the painters, from reimbursement for costs of materials all the way to a sum of many years' wages for a qualified artisan. It might have been a stimulant for many, because it contained an element of hazard: hope for great winnings, a sudden change in life's bad luck. A chance existed that one day a generous buyer would appear, a prince from a fairy tale like Cosimo who with one purchase would open perspectives of wealth. Very likely Gerard Terborch nourished such a hope in his heart when he painted "The Peace of Muenster" (1648).

The majority probably did not count on miracles. They worked by the sweat of their brows and experienced many slumps, when they had to get rid of their works for nothing.

In 1641 Adriaen's brother Isaac van Ostade, crushed by financial troubles, sold thirteen of his paintings to a merchant for the ridiculous price of 27 guldens. (Documents have transmitted the name of the extortioner.) Two guldens barely covered his costs, the price of paints and canvas. Ten guldens were sometimes paid for apprentices' copies.

In the homes of seventeenth-century Holland, even those of the middle-class and less affluent bourgeois, one could find a hundred, two hundred, and even more paintings. This was something not encountered anywhere else. When we read that a certain widow in Rotterdam liquidated the estate of her deceased husband and sold, so to say wholesale, 180 paintings for 352 guldens, a situation not very advantageous for the artist opens before us. A huge supply: there were too many cheap paintings on the market. This state of affairs was partly alleviated by the growing affluence of the upper spheres of society, their passion for collecting, and their unremitting love for Dutch painting.

We are surprised today that the paintings of the old masters Van Eyck, Memling, Quentin Matsys—splendid progenitors of Flemish art—were relatively inexpensive, and did not arouse as much interest as one might suppose. In 1654 it was possible to purchase a portrait from the brush of Jan van Eyck at well-known dealers for 18 guldens.

PAINTINGS in seventeenth-century Holland were objects of speculation, or increased exchange. They often went from hand to hand and were traded in different ways, which led some researchers to claim that in this country they became similar to money—a substitute currency. A closer analogy would be stock shares with a changeable, capricious market value, difficult to foresee.

The Dutch painter could pay for almost anything with his paintings. He often saved himself from bankruptcy or prison by getting rid of his works. Rembrandt was notorious for it; for instance he gave away to Dirck van Cattenbugh a number of paintings and sketches to cover a large debt amounting to 3,000 guldens.

Loans were secured by pledging paintings; debts (card debts as well) were paid with them, cobblers', butchers', bakers', and tailors' bills were settled with paintings. In such cases the latitude of prices was great, and the advantage of the creditor-predator evident. But exceptions occurred. The mediocre Flemish artist Matteus van Helmont, who painted in the manner of Tenier and Brouwer, was unable to pay a debt to a brewer; he gave him only one painting, "The Peasants' Wedding," and subtracted from his bill the substantial amount of 240 guldens, a sum Vermeer never obtained. The excellent Joos de Momper, who painted "impressionist" landscapes surging like a stormy sea, had an inclination for wine and visited all too often the tavern of a certain Gijsbrecht van der Cruyse. As a result, twenty-three landscapes by Momper were hung in the house of the owner of the winery in a special room, the finest in the house, upholstered in gilded leather—a collection not owned by the richest museums of the world.

Jan Steen, owner of an inn, painted a canvas for his supplier and received a barrel of wine. A certain painter of flowers who was in debt to a baker for 35 guldens gave him a painting that the baker sold for triple profit soon afterward.

With paintings it was possible to pay off a house, buy a horse, and give a dowry to a daughter if the master did not possess any other wealth. We are familiar with some of the complex, long-term contracts. A painter sells his colleague a house for the sum of 9,000 guldens. The buyer commits himself to deliver each month a painting valued at 31 guldens (a "large" one, because a middle-size painting was worth 18 guldens). If there was a delay in delivery, an agreed-upon fine was set at the amount of six guldens. The painter's supplies, paints, canvas, and frames were paid half-and-half by both sides.

Here is a peculiar agreement touching on otherworldly matters. In exchange for lower rent, a painter promised the landlord to paint the portrait of his beloved daughter, deceased years ago.

The painting of portraits (they made Rembrandt's reputation and then contributed to his fall) limited the artist's risk, because as a rule the model was the purchaser. He would ask to be immortalized in the period of his prosperity, and often the ambition to entrust this task to a good master got the better of stinginess. One had to paint full cheeks, eyes boldly looking into the future, and also the lace and satin of festive attire as exactly as possible. Everyone wants to look better and more dignified than in reality.

Sometimes painters would succumb to the amusing mythomania of their clients. The buyer who signed a contract with Jan Lievens obligated the artist to present him as Scipio Africanus and his wife as Pallas Athena. The grocery merchant Gabriel Lehencamp, with the unbridled fantasy characteristic of grocers, requested that the painter represent him as the Archangel Gabriel, and his beloved as the Madonna.

On the art market there were many mediocre paintings next to good ones and even shoddy ones (rubbish covered with a patina appears more noble to us), as well as an innumerable number of copies. After all, apprentices started their education by copying, mature masters "repeated" their own paintings, and those who were less able counterfeited the talented and fashionable painters without scruples.

In 1632 Adriaen Brouwer declared before a notary that he had made only one painting, titled "Peasants' Dance," and that the painting was in the possession of Rubens. In this way the artist wanted to cut himself off from the counterfeit Brouwers in circulation, probably a struggle with windmills. The procedure of counterfeiting paintings, as old as art itself, developed in Holland in the seventeenth century on a grand scale and with a rush.

The story we will now tell, simplified greatly, has all the elements of a picaresque novel. It could be called "The Greatness and Fall of Gerrit Uylenburgh."

Who was the hero? A painter without talent. As we know

31

from history, these can be individuals who are dangerous for those around them, especially when endowed by nature with a will to power or at least an overwhelming imperative pushing them to make a career at any price. His father Henry Uylenburgh, cousin of Rembrandt's wife Saskia, tried his hand at many jobs: he traded works of art, was an estate appraiser, cleaned and varnished. A modest, laborious, worry-filled gray life.

His son Gerrit was made of different clay. Clever, ambitious, he had a gift of winning people over and wove an intricate web of connections and acquaintances until he gained the confidence of the Republic's influential personalities. In 1660 the Estates General entrusted him with a mission of envoy to the court of the English King Charles II. As a gift for the king Gerrit carried twenty-four paintings of the Italian School purchased from a wealthy widow for the sum—by no means trivial—of 80,000 guldens.

The journey toward the shores of the island with his precious cargo decided Uylenburgh's fate. Neither sea demons nor the Great Tempter needed to trouble themselves; the temptation was born of itself in Gerrit's practical head. It took the form of a dazzlingly simple idea. There was not much sense in importing paintings from Venice or Rome, since enough artists lived in Holland who knew how to paint everything no worse and, in addition, far less expensively. The Italians had to be beaten with their own weapon. This was his war cry.

After his return to Amsterdam, Gerrit bought two houses where he arranged exhibition rooms, ateliers, and gathered artists who craved a steady income. This is how the great fabrication of Italian painting in Holland began. The whole affair was surrounded with proper discretion.

In the beginning everything developed favorably and the business flourished. Suddenly, quite unexpectedly, crafty fate threw its treacherous nets over Gerrit. It was when he signed a very profitable contract with the Prince-Elector of Brandenburg to supply him with thirteen paintings by famous Italian masters. He took an advance of 4,000 guldens. But who could have foreseen that in the prince's court at the time was a Dutch painter of flowers, Henryck Fromentin, who years ago had worked dog-cheap for the manufacturer of the Italian paintings "Made in Amsterdam." His revenge was sweet, his expertise overpowering; not a single one of the paintings was an authentic work of the Italian School.

From now on events develop at an accelerated pace. The prince sends the paintings back, the whole affair gets publicity. Outraged Gerrit calls a commission of nine experts, which pronounces a Solomon's verdict: some paintings are good, some less good, but all could be found in collections of Italian art. It is not known what this was supposed to mean. In enigmatic verdicts, as in mysterious women, a certain lack of clarity possesses its own charm.

Ambitious Gerrit is not satisfied with this resolution. For years he fiercely defends his merchant's honor and, speaking more simply, his existence.

The judgments of experts multiply. A group of specialists, among them excellent painters such as van Aelst and Kalf, categorically decides that Gerrit's entire collection is an accumulation of incompetent kitsch. On the other hand the verdict of another commission, called later on, is less emphatic; thirty-one painters speak for the authenticity of the paintings, twenty against. As with the conjectural prosecution, the contradictory opinions of experts obscure the matter even further.

The affair develops on two planes. The first is a spectacular scandal that holds the entire artistic world of Holland in suspense. Jokes, pamphlets, and poems circulate written by self-taught but also well-known poets like Vondel. They defend

Uylenburgh or pitilessly make fun of him. Let us be frank—all those who passionately like to watch public executions or bankruptcies with a bang have here a great dose of healthy entertainment.

We can guess at the hidden mainsprings of the affair on another, deeper level. How to explain the great disparity of opinion of the several score Dutch painters who took part in the appraisal? Was it not a trial *in absentia* of the art of the Italians, who were a dangerous, unbeatable competition for the native artists?

At last Gerrit is forced to capitulate. In 1674, he auctions his "Italian" paintings, and two years later sells the rest of his collection, which includes excellent paintings by Rembrandt, Lastmann, van Aelst, Metsu, and Hercules Seghers. All of them are authentic beyond any doubt.

Uylenburgh leaves his ungrateful homeland. He departs for England—that is, the place of his great temptation. Thanks to the generosity of an English colleague, he will paint landscape backgrounds for portraits until the end of his life.

Ars alit artificem. Like all golden thoughts and sentences from almanacs, this one should be treated with a proper dose of skepticism. If art indeed nourishes artists, it is a mannered, absentminded, and often completely unpredictable nourisher.

The Dutch painters of the "golden age" undertook all kinds of employment that a contemporary so-called artist would reject as degrading. They were artisans, and their humility toward life was great and beautiful.

Several of the other occupations had something in common with their profession, requiring competence with a brush and knowledge of materials, though these went beyond the frames of paintings. They painted everything: ceilings, pictures on mantelpieces, frontons, they decorated ships, carriages, spinets, clocks, tiles, ceramics, and painted shop signs on order. The good painter Gerrit Berckheyde was christened the Ra-

34

phael of signboards. A French traveler, Sorbier, admired the aesthetic appearance of Dutch shops "dont les enseignes sont quelquefois de fort bons tableaux." Carel Fabritius patched up his home budget by painting municipal coats of arms at 212 guldens apiece.

Others, the best known painters among them, led a "double" professional life. They were cooks, innkeepers, owners of taverns or brick kilns, petty clerks, traders of works of art, real estate, stockings, tulips, and whatever was at hand.

The smile of fortune, the grace of fate, occurs more often in affluent countries, where everyone quietly counts on it. Gerard Dou, that lucky charmer, received 500 guldens a year from the Swedish envoy in The Hague for the right of purchase alone.

The good reputation of Dutch painters secured invitations to foreign courts, so Godfried Schalcken, Adriaen van der Werff, and Eglon van der Neer, for example, spent years in the service of the Prince Elector in Dusseldorf. But the great ones—Vermeer, Hals, Rembrandt—never traveled to the other side of the Alps, or even neighboring countries. They remained faithful to the trees, walls, clouds of their homeland, and to their native towns. What is stranger still, this provincialism by choice constituted their strength, and decided their posthumous triumph.

Lack of stability, the uncertainty of tomorrow were the artists' curse. They tried to remedy it in different ways, and to secure a stable means of existence for some period of time. Only a few succeeded. A highly valued painter, Emmanuel de Witte, signed a contract with a notary, Joris de Wijs, giving his entire yearly production in exchange for 800 guldens and room and board. It happened that a rich merchant or collector setting out on a voyage to France or Italy would take an artist with him who for a set sum sketched landscapes, unusual attractions, and town sights.

We have tried to look at the life of seventeenth-century Dutch painters from the banal and not very striking point of view of the balance sheet: "he owes," "he has"—that is, petty bookkeeping. It is better and more honest than the pathos and sentimental sighs favored by authors of *vies romancées* written for tender hearts.

It is true that fate did not spare the members of the Guild of Saint Luke. We know that Hercules Seghers and the seventy-five-year-old Emmanuel de Witte, overwhelmed by material difficulties, committed suicide. Hals, Hobbema, and Ruysdael died in the poorhouse. Poverty and alcoholism occurred often, but not always. The excellent Philips Wouwerman gave his daughter 20,000 guldens as a dowry; the Marinist Jan de Cappelle could rest in peace because he left an estate valued at 100,000 guldens, a splendid collection of two hundred paintings (among others, Rubens, van Dyke, Rembrandt), and several thousand drawings. It should be added, however, that Cappelle drew his income to a greater degree from a prospering dye-works than from his painting.

Information preserved about the lives of the Dutch painters is sparse. They belong to that species of artists who leave works behind them, not complaints and laments. Really there are no dramatic stories, unhealthy blushing, or sensational scandals. Their entirely earthly existence can be summarized in a few dates: birth, qualification as a master, marriage, children's baptism, and finally death.

They can only be envied. Whatever their greatness and miseries, the disillusionments and failures of their careers, their role in society and place on earth were not questioned, their profession universally recognized and as evident as the profession of butcher, tailor, or baker. The question why art exists did not occur to anyone, because a world without paintings was simply inconceivable.

It is we who are poor, very poor. A major part of contemporary art declares itself on the side of chaos, gesticulates in a void, or tells the story of its own barren soul.

The old masters—all of them without exception—could repeat after Racine, "We work to please the public." Which means they believed in the purposefulness of their work and the possibility of interhuman communication. They affirmed visible reality with an inspired scrupulousness and childish seriousness, as if the order of the world and the revolution of the stars, the permanence of the firmament, depended on it.

Let such naïveté be praised.

THE BITTER SMELL
OF TULIPS

❏

... galant tulip will hang down his head
like to a virgin newly ravished ...
—ROBERT HERRICK

1.

HERE is a story of human folly.

It is not about fire consuming a great city on a river, nor the slaughter of defenseless people. It is not about a vast plain bathed in morning light where armed riders meet other riders to find out which of the two commanders will earn at the end of the day, after a murderous battle, a modest place in history, a monument of bronze, or, with less luck, give his name to an alleyway in some suburb of poverty.

Our drama is modest and with little pathos, far from the famous hemorrhages of history. Because everything began innocently—with a plant, a flower, a tulip (this is hard to imagine) that unleashed collective, uncontrollable passions. Further, for those who have studied the phenomenon the most amazing thing was that this folly shook a sober, hard-working, and parsimonious nation. The question arises: How did it happen that in enlightened Holland and not somewhere else, *tulpenwoede*—tulipomania—reached such frightening dimensions, shook the foundations of a solid national economy, and drew representatives of all social levels into a gigantic frenzy of gambling?

Some explain it with the proverbial love of the Netherlanders for flowers. An old anecdote recounts that a lady requested an artist to paint a bouquet of rare flowers for her because she could not afford to buy them. This is how a new and so far unknown branch of painting came into being. Let us stress that for this lady, inspirer of a new genre in art, aesthetic motives played a totally secondary role. What she wanted most was a real object: a crown of petals on a green stem. The artist's work was a mere substitute, a shadow of existing things. Similarly, lovers doomed to separation must be content with the likeness of a beloved face. In the beginning the painting expresses nostalgia for a faraway and unreachable lost reality.

There are other reasons, more prosaic and down-to-earth, that sufficiently explain the peculiar Dutch predilection for flowers. Deprived of luxuriant, exuberant vegetation and disciplined by a rational economy, the country amazed many travelers because they found no humming wheatfields there. Wheat was imported from abroad. There was little land, its quality often poor, while the price was always exorbitant. Most arable land was devoted to pastures, orchards, and gardens. The nature of the country required an intensive economy of land that was spatially restricted.

Nature also challenges man aesthetically, so it is not difficult to understand that a certain monotony of the Dutch landscape gave rise to dreams of multifarious, colorful, and unusual flora. Possibly the nostalgia for a lost paradise lurked behind it, which medieval painters represented in the form of a rosarium, an orchard, or a flower bed. Eternal greenness speaks to the imagination better than eternal light.

In comparison with the pompous splendor of the gardens of French or English lords, the equivalents in Holland were of course modest. Most often they occupied the space of barely several score square feet. But what a wealth of plants, what conscious composition of colors. A lawn with islands of moss and patches of multicolored flowers, lilac bushes and an apple tree, a pattern imposed on all of it and a network of lilliputian paths strewn with white sand.

Everyone, even a simple artisan, wished to own a flower bed at the back of his house and cultivate roses, irises, lilies, and hyacinths that are more beautiful, more unusual than those in his neighbor's garden. This adoration of nature, like an echo of the most remote vegetative cults, had all the attributes of enlightened love. Eminent connoisseurs of the world of plants lectured in Leyden and other universities—for instance the Frenchman Lecluse, called Clusius (more about him later on), who founded the first botanical garden in 1587. Scholars set out with colonists on distant, dangerous expeditions to learn the secrets of exotic nature. The public at large avidly read books devoted to the classification, anatomy, and cultivation of plants. The summa of this rich literature is a fat, three-volume work by Jan van der Meurs with the telling title *Arboretum Sacrum*.

In the Mauritshuis in The Hague there is a canvas, "Bouquet against a Vaulted Window," by an excellent painter of flowers, Ambrosius Bosschaert the Elder. This painting always fills me with a kind of anxiety, although I realize its cause is not the subject chosen by the painter. For what is more soothing, more idyllic than an arrangement of roses, dahlias, irises, and orchids presented with sophisticated simplicity against a background of sky and a distant mountainous landscape fading into the blue?

Yet the treatment of the subject is striking and somewhat eerie. The flowers in this painting—quiet servants of nature, and helpless givers of delight—flaunt themselves; they are exclusive sovereigns who domineer with an intensity and force never encountered until then. It seems that an important and decisive act of liberation has occurred here. The "quiet servants of nature" abandon their role of ornament: they do not try to be graceful; they don't languish, but attack the spectator with their proud, one wants to say their self-conscious, individuality. They seem overnatural, insistently present. All of this happens not because they are an expression of violent, internal states of the artist (like Van Gogh's "Sunflowers"), but quite the opposite. The shape, color, and character of the flowers have been reproduced scrupulously, in detail, with the cold impartiality of a botanist and anatomist. The light of the painting, clear and "objective," means that the artist has abandoned all the charms of chiaroscuro and the painterly hierarchy that plunges some objects in shadow and accentuates others by lighting. The "Bouquet against a Vaulted Window" can be compared to Frans Hals's collective portraits in which there is no division into persons who are more important or less.

Bosschaert's painting was made around 1620, shortly before the artist's death. The events we are about to relate took place several years later. But already in this painting it is possible to notice omens of an approaching storm. For aren't these emancipated, dominating, rapacious flowers, loudly demanding admiration and praise, a symptom of a peculiar cult? The composition of the painting indicates this. The bouquet is placed on a high window as if on an altar, elevated above the rest of nature. A pagan monstrance of flowers.

In Bosschaert's painting—auguring nothing good—are a few tulips.

2.

It is not at all unlikely that illnesses have their
history, and every epoch has its own definite sickness
which did not occur in such guise before, and will
never again return in the same form.

—TROELS-LUND

THE tulip is a gift from the East, like so many other blessed
and ominous gifts: religions and superstitions, medicinal and
intoxicating herbs, holy books and invasions, epidemics and
fruit. Its name comes from Persian and designates a turban.
For centuries it was a favorite and honored flower in the gardens of Armenia, Turkey, and Persia. At the sultan's courts a
tulip holiday was celebrated every year. The poets Omar
Khayyam and Hafiz sang its praises, it is mentioned in the
tales of *The Thousand and One Nights;* before it traveled to Europe it had a long Oriental career of many years behind it.

Its appearance in the West was the contribution of a diplomat. He was Ogier Gheslin de Busbeq, envoy of the Austrian
Hapsburgs at the court of Suleiman the Magnificent in Con-
stantinople. An educated man and curious about the world
(his interesting travel descriptions have been preserved), he
dutifully wrote comprehensive diplomatic reports. But it
seems he had far greater enthusiasm for collecting Greek
manuscripts, ancient inscriptions, and naturalia. In 1554 he
sent a transport of tulip bulbs to the Viennese court of
the Emperor Francis I. Such was the innocent beginning of
the evil.

From this time on the flower's popularity spread in Europe
with surprising speed. Konrad Gesner, called the German
Pliny, gave the first scientific description of the plant in his
work *De Hortis Germaniae* (1561). In the same year guests of
the banker family Fugger admired patches of this still rare

flower at their gardens in Augsburg. A little later it appears in France, the Netherlands, and England, where John Trandescent, gardener of Charles I, boasted of cultivating fifty varieties of tulip. For a short period gastronomers tried to make a delicacy out of it for elegant tables: in Germany it was eaten with sugar. In England, on the other hand, it was spiced with oil and vinegar. The infamous conspiracy of pharmacists to make a medicine against flatulence from this plant also luckily came to nothing. The tulip remained itself, the poetry of Nature to which vulgar utilitarianism is foreign.

Thus in the beginning it was a flower of monarchs, of the well-born, the wealthy—very precious, carefully kept in gardens, and inaccessible. Contemporaries invented a soul for it; they said it expressed elegance and refined meditation. Even its infirmity—its lack of smell—was interpreted as the virtue of moderation. One could indeed say that cold beauty has an introverted character. The tulip allows us to admire it but does not awaken violent emotions, desire, jealousy, or erotic fervors. It is a peacock among flowers; at any rate, this is what the courtly "philosophers of gardens" wrote. History proved that they erred.

It is well known that court fashions are contagious; also they are often imitated by the lower classes, and for this they meet a well-deserved divine punishment. In the beginning of the seventeenth century, chroniclers in France observed the first symptoms—let us put it this way—of acute tulip fever. In 1608 a miller parted with his mill for a single bulb of a rarely encountered variety called "Mère brune." A young groom was supposedly enchanted when his father-in-law gave him a single precious plant as his entire dowry, appropriately called for the occasion "Mariage de ma fille." Another enthusiast did not hesitate to exchange his flourishing brewery for a bulb, which since that time carries the not very elegant name "Tulipe brasserie."

One could multiply examples without difficulty to prove

that wherever the tulip appeared cases of tulipomania were registered, sometimes more, sometimes less. But only in Holland did it reach the intensity and dimensions of an epidemic.

Its beginnings are unclear and difficult to establish precisely, both in terms of time and of space. With the plague the matter is much simpler: One day a ship from the East puts in at a harbor. Part of the crew has a high fever; some are delirious, and tumors can be seen on their bodies. They go ashore and are put in hospitals, houses, and inns; the first deaths occur, and the number of fatal illnesses rapidly grows. The entire city, the entire region, the entire country is swept by plague. Princes and beggars, saints and freethinkers, criminals and innocent children all die. Since the time of Thucydides this pandemonium of death has been described many times and in detail.

On the other hand, tulipomania is a mental phenomenon, and here the troubles begin. In other words, it is a social psychosis like other psychoses, whether associated with religion, war, revolution, or the economy—for instance, gold fever or the crash of the American stock market in 1929. Despite numerous, striking analogies, it cannot of course be explained in terms of infectious diseases (but what a pity!). We lack instruments that would allow us to measure quantitatively the range of the epidemic, its degree of "infectiousness," the number with an acute or mild sickness, "the temperature curve" of affected individuals. The only method left is to enter into the spirit of the events, a cautious description that notes both the extreme and characteristic cases.

It is not possible to define exactly when the tulip appeared for the first time in the Netherlands. Most likely it was quite early. We know, for example, that in 1562 a shipment of tulip bulbs was received in the port of Antwerp. But the intensive interest in the flower occurred many years later, most likely reflecting the fashion reigning at the royal courts, especially the French. At the end of the sixteenth century something happened that on the surface seems an unimportant case from police chronicles but in fact was one of the first symptoms of tulipomania on Dutch soil. We have already mentioned Carolus Clusius, professor of botany at the famous university in Leyden (he previously held the rank of Director of the Imperial Gardens in Vienna). This scholar was widely known, at the same time talkative and possibly somewhat vain. At every occasion he talked about the plants he was cultivating, not only to university colleagues but also to chance listeners. Usually he spoke with enthusiasm and unconcealed pride about the tulips, which, he claimed, he would not exchange for any of the world's treasures. It was an open provocation, which the scholar probably did not realize. One night—let us say moonless—unknown persons forced their way into the university gardens and stole Clusius's tulips. The thieves must have had considerable scientific qualifications, because their loot was exclusively the precious and truly rare tulip varieties. The embittered botanist stopped studying this plant till the end of his life.

The story recalls the ballad about the sorcerer's apprentice. A sudden transmutation occurs: the object of patient, scholarly, and therefore disinterested studies is transformed into an object of insane financial transactions. An important question comes to mind here: Why precisely was it the tulip, and not another flower, that liberated the madness?

There were several reasons. We already noted that the tulip was an aristocratic, almost worshiped flower. What a pleasure to possess something that was the pride of monarchs! Aside from snobbish considerations, there were also reasons that might be called purely biological, for the cultivation of a tulip did not involve any large problems or troubles. It was a grateful flower, easy to tame. Everyone who owned even the smallest patch of earth could give himself up to the passion.

In Dutch gardens a certain kind of virus was rife that often caused the petals of the tulip's crown to take on fantastic shapes with ruffled or pleated edges. It was quickly learned how to draw a profit from this pathology.

Finally, and this is particularly important for our thoughts on the scientific basis of tulipomania, no other flower possessed such a quantity of varieties. People were convinced that this plant had a peculiar property: sooner or later it would produce spontaneously—that is, without man's participation—new mutations, and new multicolored forms. It was said nature particularly cherished this flower, and endlessly played with it. To speak in a less ornate way, it meant that the buyer of a tulip bulb was in a situation like a man playing a lottery: blind chance could bestow a large fortune on him.

In the first half of the seventeenth century, the Dutch took pride in three things: a powerful and invincible navy, "the sweets of freedom greater than anywhere else," and—if one may combine important and unimportant matters in a single sentence—at least several hundred varieties of tulips. It seems the dictionary could not keep pace with this wealth of nature. We have simultaneously five kinds of "Miracle," four "Emeralds," as many as thirty "Paragons of Perfection" (a semantic abuse of the word). Those endowed with fantasy invented names full of poetry—"Royal Agate," "Diana," and "Harlequin"—while those deprived of imagination called their specimens simply "Gaudy," "Virgin," or "Yellow-Red." To cope with the growing task, military ranks were introduced and even history was harnessed, so we have "Admiral van Enckhuysen," "General van Eyck," and many others. A certain clever cultivator boldly decided to bid higher, calling his variety "General of Generals." There is, of course, "King," "Vice-King," and "Prince," as if someone wanted to introduce military and aristocratic order into this multifariousness bordering on chaos.

The huge quantity of tulip varieties that Holland managed to cultivate stirs our admiration and bewilderment, but it contained the seeds of catastrophe as well. If a game uses a small number of cards as a rule it is simple, banal, and quickly ends. However, when the players dispose of let's say several decks of cards, the field is open to complex combinations, intelligent strategy, a balanced risk, and shrewd methods. The same happened with tulips; one had only to agree which varieties would have the value of an "ace" and which would be counted among "minnows."

Of course this is a greatly simplified scheme, a first, timid approach to the subject. Ludic elements undoubtedly played a role. But in fact tulipomania was a very complex phenomenon. It seems the most decisive and important aspect of the problem was economic; in other words, the order of the stock market was introduced into the order of nature. The tulip began to lose the properties and charms of a flower: it grew pale, lost its colors and shapes, became an abstraction, a name, a symbol interchangeable with a certain amount of money. Complicated tables existed on which individual varieties were arranged according to the changing market prices like valuable papers or money rates. The hour of the great speculation had struck.

During the entire period of tulipomania, which lasted several years, "Semper Augustus" invariably remained at the top of these price lists, like a sun standing motionless at the zenith. I never personally encountered it. It is vain to look for it in flower shops, which like all our other shops sell standard roses, standard eggs, standard cars. My fault. If I visited botanical gardens as assiduously as museums, the meeting might have occurred. I know this tulip, however, from old, colorful engravings; it is indeed beautiful, thanks to its sophisticated and at the same time simple harmony of colors: petals impeccably white, and with small, fiery, ruby veins running along

47

them, the bottom of the chalice blue like the reflection of a sunny sky. It is an exceptionally nice specimen, but the price reached by "Semper Augustus," 5,000 florins (the equivalent of a house with a large garden), causes a shiver of anxiety. The dikes of common sense had broken. From now on we will move on the slippery terrain of unhealthy fantasy, feverish desire for profit, insane illusions, and bitter disappointments.

Transactions were often made in kind. These allow us to measure the dimensions of the madness even better. For a bulb of the tulip "Vice-King" (it was worth half the value of "Semper Augustus"), the following was paid in the form of farm products:

> 2 carts of wheat
> 4 carts of rye
> 4 fat oxen
> 8 fat pigs
> 12 fat sheep
> 2 barrels of wine
> 4 barrels of the foremost beer
> 1,000 pounds of cheese

A bed, clothes, and a silver chalice were added to this drink, food, and fatness.

In the initial phase of tulipomania, prices went constantly up. As stockbrokers would say, the trend on the "flower stock market" was at first "friendly," then "lively," all the way to "very lively," to pass in the end to a state of euphoria completely uncontrolled by common sense.

A greater and greater gap opened between the real value of the plants sold and the price paid for them. It was paid willingly, with joy, as if expecting the smile of fate. Most of those touched by tulipomania counted on a boom; they were convinced the rising trend would continue forever (don't they resemble the progressives?), and that a bulb bought today would double its value tomorrow or at the latest the day after tomorrow. If one treats these fantastic speculations seriously and without irony (because "seniority" in history does not entitle one to it), we can see something more profound—for instance, the old myth of humanity about miraculous multiplication.

In earthly categories the matter looked as follows: the sellers took no account at all of the actual possibilities of the buyers, and what is worse the buyers seemed to have entirely lost the instinct of self-preservation. They were no longer aware of their own possibilities. The hectic atmosphere that accompanies large stock operations is universally known, but in the case of tulipomania it was something more serious and more pathological than an "atmosphere."

The psychological deviations defined as manias possess certain common features. The persons affected by the disease have a tendency to create imaginary, autonomous worlds governed by their own rules. In our case it was like a gigantic flower lottery, and all those who played expected the first prize. The game, however, did not take place on an island especially leased for the purpose, but in a country where the cardinal virtues were caution, moderation, and accountability. A system based on bourgeois calculation could not coexist with a system of financial phantasmagoria. The collison of the world of desires with everyday reality was inevitable, and as is usual in such cases, painful.

It is worthwhile now to ponder in what way, in what places, and in what social framework the speculation in tulip bulbs took place. The answer closest to the truth would be: on the margin of normal economic life, in its dark corners, so to say. Several times we have mentioned the stock market, but this should not be taken literally. There never was and there could not be an official tulip stock market, because this institution assumes openness, admits a limited number of those authorized to take part, and the results of transactions are announced to all who are interested.

On the other hand, we know the wild commerce in tulips caused the authorities to be seriously worried and alarmed. Orders were given to limit and curb, if not eliminate, this dangerous social phenomenon. But these did not help much; strictly speaking their effect was the opposite of what was intended. The elements cannot be calmed by gentle persuasion.

The country lived in fever. Whoever remembers war knows very well that the most fantastic, unverified information is capable of pulling people from the bottom of despair and transporting them to towering heights of optimism, of illusory hopes. A similar thing happened in our case. News of sudden fortunes achieved because of the tulips spread with the speed of lightning. A citizen of Amsterdam who owned a small garden earned 60,000 florins in four months, a wealth not dreamed of by an average merchant even at the end of a laborious life. An Englishman who knew nothing about flowers managed to make five thousand pounds by ingenious speculations. One had to have a stoic character indeed to resist these temptations.

Because the whole procedure was unofficial and even had the character of a forbidden game, it became more attractive for precisely this reason, drawing ever new participants. It was like a period of prohibition when those with only a moderate liking for intoxicants manifest their freedom by excessive consumption of alcohol.

There are of course no statistics that show how many people were touched by tulipomania. But it is possible, even probable, that they numbered in the tens of thousands. What is particularly important, they cannot be assigned to any single, specific social group. Among them were the wealthy and the poor, merchants and weavers, butchers and students, painters and peasants, peat diggers and poets, city clerks and junk dealers, sailors and virtuous widows, persons generally respected and criminals. Even the followers of all twenty or more religious denominations took unanimous part in this race for fortune. The poor risked most of all—the poor risked everything. When we read that a criminal drawn into the whirlpool of speculations pawned his tools, we realize the full horror of the situation. Preachers thundered from their pulpits against wicked tulipomania, but the malicious maintained that they slipped away to other cities where they could succumb to the sinful craze without unwanted witnesses.

But never mind the pastors. They will always find some excuse at the Last Judgment. What is worse, or frankly disgraceful, is that children were drawn into the action. Success in the game required among other things collecting the greatest possible amount of information—prices, places of transaction, fluctuations of the market. In simple language, to know which tulip bulbs the neighbor hid under his jacket and for how much he sold them in the tavern At the Braying Donkey, all of it had to be found out by a teenager performing the vile function of spy.

Fever, raving, and sleeplessness. Sleeplessness, because many tulip transactions were sealed at night. Active participation in speculating often swallowed up many hours of the day, and could not be combined with other more productive occupations. Those who cultivated tulips lived like misers in a sack of gold. Ingenious systems of alarm bells were installed in gardens to rouse the owner to his feet if an uninvited guest approached his patch.

The epidemic character of tulipomania explains its enormous geographic range. It touched not only the traditional garden districts—for instance the regions of Haarlem, but also Amsterdam, Alkmar, Hoorn, Enkhuizen, Utrecht, Rotterdam—that is, all the greater conglomerations in Holland. It is precisely there that the number of victims was the highest. The bacillus of tulipomania was everywhere in the air, and threatened everyone. How much easier it is to dispose of a visible enemy: the gates of the city are closed, the brave defenders go out onto the walls . . .

But after all, something exists that we call the power of reason, and it is an effective weapon (not always) against unbridled irrational powers. We know that Holland was a country of people who liked to read, with wise authors, educated booksellers, and enlightened publishers. Actual problems would meet a response in print very quickly; this was true not only of serious political and religious disputes. The affair of tulipomania, whose dimensions awoke understandable anxiety, also met with decisive resistance and protests from sober citizens. But the country was liberal; public opinion differentiated. Together with voices of reason, pamphlets appeared that were practical introductions to the principles of tulip speculation, prolegomena to insanity: teach-yourself manuals on how to become a madman.

In all of it there was a method, and even a ritual. One author recommended that if someone succeeded in cultivating an unknown variety of tulip he should act as follows: immediately go to a professional gardener (time presses, because someone else might have managed a similar trick), not alone but accompanied by acquaintances, friends, even persons encountered by chance. The goal was evident: to give the greatest possible publicity to the event. A council took place at the gardener's, each person present expressing his opinion about the botanical revelation—exactly like high church councils preoccupied with the problems of real and imaginary miracles.

Now a very important step followed. We could call it comparative: the consideration of the new variety side by side with others that were already known. If it showed similarity to some famous "Admiral" but was less beautiful, it should be modestly called "General." This ritual of baptism was incredibly important. The tulip became a personality, or to speak less grandiloquently and use stock-market terminology, a value admitted into circulation. In the end it was proper to offer a fine wine to all those present, because it was up to them to spread the news about the birth of a new variety, to praise its graces.

Transactions with tulip bulbs would take place in the fumes of beer, gin, and lamb, in restaurants, inns, and taverns. Some of them had rooms specially designated for this purpose; they were a kind of club, or branches of a huge and well-concealed stock market. The fight for each precious variety of tulip must have been fierce. If several buyers competed for it, the one who wanted to outbid others would add to an already excessive price a carriage with a pair of horses.

The entire country was covered by a network of more or less known, secret, or almost open gambling "dens" for tulips. It did not involve any demonic power but the simple rule of every "big game," every powerful addiction—to draw in and entrap the greatest possible number of people. Because madness cannot be logically justified, it is necessary to have strong statistics in one's defense. This is what everybody does, or almost everybody, including politicians: to eliminate or substantially decrease the number of those who stand aside, who look on or observe critically and spoil the game. The world of tulipomaniacs strove to become a total world.

How did it happen in practice? A document exists, literary to be sure but trustworthy, which provides precious information about the means of capturing new enthusiasts. A dialogue takes place between two friends. The first, Pieter, is an expert speculator; the second, Jan, plays the role of a novice in this conversation:

PIETER: I like you very much. This is why I want to propose to you this advantageous transaction. I do it without any self-interest, and out of pure friendship.

JAN: I am listening carefully, my dear friend.

PIETER: I have a bulb of the tulip "Harlequin." It is a very beautiful variety, and in addition much sought after on the market.

JAN: But I never had anything to do with flowers in my whole life. I don't even have a garden.

PIETER: You don't understand a thing. Please listen to me; don't interrupt because who knows, maybe today a great fortune is knocking at your door. Can I go on?

JAN: Yes, yes, of course.

PIETER: Well, the "Harlequin" bulb is worth a hundred florins, and maybe even more. In the name of our unblemished (as I said) friendship, I will let you have it for fifty florins. Still today, without any effort, you can make quite a lot of money.

JAN: This is indeed a splendid proposition. Nothing like this has ever happened to me before. Only tell me, please, what am I to do with this "Harlequin"? After all, I will not stand at the street corner . . .

PIETER: I will tell you the whole secret. But note it down well in your memory. Why are you fidgeting?

JAN: I am listening, only I am a bit dizzy.

PIETER: Do exactly as I say. Go to the inn At the Lion. Ask the innkeeper where the tulip vendors meet. You will enter the room he indicates. Then someone will say in a very thick voice (but don't you be put off by it): "A stranger has come in." In answer to that, cluck like a chicken. From that moment on you will be included in the community of vendors.

May God protect Jan's Calvinist soul! We part with him on the threshold of farce and a step away from tragedy. Darkness covers his future fate. It is not even known whether he managed to cluck in an appropriate and persuasive manner at the decisive moment. On the basis of this tale there is little hope he would become a shark of the tulip stock market. It seems he was assigned the role of victim.

One more detail merits our attention. This introduction to the trade of the tulipomaniacs reminds us of patterns known from other areas. Keeping all proportions in mind, it recalls the ritual of initiation. Of course the Masonic lodges arranged it with greater pomp and better knowledge of esoteric science. Mania is an elevated state of mind. Those who have not experienced it at least once are the poorer for it. Besides, in certain conditions it brings advantages. An ordinary man who was unknown to anyone—he was neither a poet nor painter nor statesman—recalled with genuine sentiment the times of the tulipomania. His name was Waermondt; he held office always in the same tavern, and his function was that of broker. Between one transaction and another, "I ate fried meat and fish, chicken and hare, even delicate pâtés. I also drank wine and beer from early morning till three or four at night. I always carried more money away at night than I had at the beginning of the day." A true Shlarafia, land of laziness and plenty.

3.

"La maladie infectueuse tend à la fois à se perpétuer et, pour assurer cette perpétuité, à se modifier suivant les circonstances."
—CHARLES NICOLLE

THE greatest intensity of tulipomania fell during the years 1634 to 1637. The great crash took place in the winter of 1637—the whole imaginary world fell apart. If someone managed to reproduce "the curve of the tulip fever," it would closely resemble the temperature chart of a patient with a serious infectious disease. The line rises fast, continues for some time on a very high level, and at the end falls rapidly.

A question comes to mind, however: What fate, or implacable logic of events, caused it to happen exactly in the winter of 1637? There are many answers.

Some believe that the victory over the tulip epidemic was the merit of the healthy portion of Dutch society. It created a sanitary belt that blocked the spread of the illness. There were those who actively opposed tulipomania; the opposition must have been quite strong since a number of brochures, magazines, pamphlets, satires, and cartoons from those times—they have been preserved until today—pitilessly make fun of the unfortunate maniacs. In colloquial language they were called "the hooded ones" or madmen; in those times the mentally ill wore hoods drawn over their faces, a peculiar device for "visual" protection of the healthy part of the nation.

Henrick Pot, a painter of collective portraits, religious and genre pictures, represented the mania afflicting his country under a veil of transparent allegory in his work "The Cart of Madmen." On this cart we recognize Flora holding in her hand three of the most precious varieties of tulip: "Semper Augustus," "General Bol," and "Admiral Hoorn." Behind the patron of nature there are five symbolic figures: Good-for-Nothing, Wealth-Craver, the Drunkard, and two ladies, Vain Hope and Poverty. A huge crowd of people runs after the cart calling, "We too want to sell our tulips."

A countless number of stories, anecdotes, and jokes show that tulipomania was answered with a decided tulipophobia, an unrelenting hostility to what was, after all, an innocent plant. In fact it deserved neither frantic adoration nor boundless spite, but we are speaking of times rocked by passions. It was said that a professor of Leyden University, Fortius, not a theologian but a professor of botany, attacked a tulip whenever he saw one, destroying it with his cane. In this unrefined manner he transformed himself from scholar into inquisitor and moralist.

Fortius's cane did not possess magic power, and even the most vicious pamphlets could not tame the insanity. Some maintain that the mortal blow to tulipomania was dealt by the authorities, with their wise orders and decrees. They realized the situation was serious and could not be looked at passively, because limitless speculation threatens the foundations of a national economy.

A number of institutions, from the florists' guild all the way up to the Estates General, or parliament, decided to oppose the folly. Instructions and resolutions poured from them, at first hesitant and inefficient but continuing all the way to the drastic decree of the Estates in April 1637, that annulled all speculative agreements and established a maximum value for a tulip bulb. It was 50 florins. "Semper Augustus" was now worth one-hundredth of its recent market price. This happened quickly and unexpectedly, like a palace revolution, like the dethronement of an emperor.

The authorities' efforts to overcome tulipomania, their concern about the fate and wealth of the citizens, are worthy of praise and of course should be fully appreciated. It seems, however, that the majority of scholars are mistaken when they ascribe to them a decisive role. We know from experience that all bans and prohibitions in cases of acute narcomania bring results that are the opposite of those intended. Ever since Paradise, the fruit that is forbidden is the most desired.

The decision of the Estates General was made late, very late, when the mania was already dying out. It was, therefore, a council gathered at the bed of a patient who was hopelessly ill, or to use an expression taken from the lexicon of tauromachy a coup de grâce. Indeed, nothing could be saved any longer.

In our opinion, tulipomania was killed by its own madness. Proofs supporting the thesis are provided by an analysis of the changing moods of the tulip market. In the period of euphoria the profits of the speculators were huge; however, they were not always expressed in negotiable currency or liquid money, but in credit. The owner of the variety "Semper Augustus" was universally considered to be a wealthy man; consequently he could borrow large amounts, and this is what he did most of the time. The crazy turnover of the market became more and more abstract. What was sold was no longer the bulbs (their value was absolutely arbitrary, further and further removed from reality and common sense), but the names of bulbs. Like shares, they often changed owners ten times a day.

Prices rose. It was expected that they would grow endlessly, because such is the logic of mania. A large number of the wary accumulated "values" in order to throw them on the market at the most propitious moment. It was precisely these cautious ones—as usually happens with greedy people entangled in the nets of gambling—who suffered the most painful defeat. Faith in the bright future of tulipomania broke down already in 1636. The edifice of trust and rampant illusions caved in. The supply of tulips was larger and larger, the demand frightfully diminishing; at the end everyone wanted to sell, but there were no bold risk takers any longer. Henrick Pot represented this phase of tulipomania accurately; the desperate cry of the crowd running after Flora's vehicle becomes quite clear in this context.

Thus the crisis had far outpaced the intervention of the authorities. On the third of January 1637, four months before the decree of the Estates General, an Amsterdam gardener bought a precious tulip bulb for a bargain price of 1,250 florins. At first happy, he soon found that he could not sell it for even half or even one-tenth of his own cost. For a sharp drop had now begun, and the game was not to make money but lose as little as possible. The entire story of this unfortunate affair extends between two poles—a long, desperate assault upon fortune, and a sudden wild panic.

We are parting thus with tulipomania, and it is a separation full of tears, curses, and moans. The statement that it could not have happened otherwise is small consolation for the victims.

What was the outcome? Because everything took place secretly, on the margins—in dark corridors and in the underground of official life—it is difficult to evaluate the dimensions of the catastrophe in measurable terms. But the outcome was without any doubt tragic: thousands of ruined estates, tens of thousands of people without work and, in addition, threatened by trials. Bankruptcy was punished, as a rule, with severe prison sentences. There were legions who had lightheartedly gone into debt. Finally—no statistics account for it—a long list of innocent families deprived of means of existence, children doomed to poverty or public charity, broken careers, destroyed reputations and dignity. The bankrupts did not have many ways out: joining the merchant marine and navy, which required certain qualifications, or begging, which did not require any special talents.

It does not need to be argued that it was an "exclusively" bourgeois tragedy. But the scale of the passions of the flower speculators equaled the scale of a heroic tenor in an opera. The aria of the stockbrokers was loud and trivial, that is evident. If we are to drag this theatrical analogy out by the hair even further, it was played without sword or blood, even without poison. Why on earth, then, does it move the imagination?

Throughout all the periods of tulipomania, not only during its fatal epilogue but during the days of its victorious euphoria, small and great human dramas were occurring. Among the many that memory has preserved we select one, a theme that might be taken straight from Chekhov's stories.

The union of florists in Haarlem became alarmed by sensational news that gripped everyone with feverish excitement: a poor, unknown shoemaker from The Hague was growing an unusual variety of tulip called "Black Tulip." It was decided to act immediately—that is, to check the matter on the spot and as far as possible to obtain the specimen. Five gentlemen dressed in black entered the dark cubbyhole of the shoemaker. They began commercial negotiations—very strange negotiations, because the gentlemen from Haarlem were playing the role of benefactors. Supposedly they had come there out of pure philanthropy to help the poor artisan, but at the same time they were unable to conceal how much they cared to possess the "Black Tulip." The master of last and leather took in the situation, and tried to get the highest price. After much haggling a transaction finally took place: 1,500 florins, not a trifling sum. A moment of happiness for the poor shoemaker.

Now something unexpected happened, something that in drama is called a turning point. The merchants threw down the bulb bought at such a high price and in fury trampled it to a pulp. "You idiot"—they shouted at the stupefied shoe-patcher—"we also have a bulb of the 'Black Tulip.' Besides us, no one else in the world! No king, no emperor or sultan. If you had asked ten thousand florins for your bulb and a couple of horses on top of it, we would have paid without a word. And remember this. Good fortune won't smile on you a second time in your entire life, because you are a blockhead." They left. The shoemaker staggered, dragged himself to his attic, lay down on his bed and, covering himself with his coat, breathed his last breath.

TULIPOMANIA—the most extraordinary botanical folly we know—was an episode inscribed on the margin of Great History. We have chosen it not without reason. It should be honestly confessed: we have a strange liking for presenting follies in the sanctuaries of reason, and we also like to study catastrophes against a gentle landscape. There are reasons more important than frivolous personal or aesthetic inclinations, however. For doesn't the affair we have described remind us of other, more dangerous follies of humanity that consist in the irrational attachment to a single idea, a single symbol, or a single formula for happiness?

This is why we cannot put a large period after the date 1637 and consider the matter definitively closed. It is not reasonable to erase it from memory, or count it among the inconceivable fads of the past. If tulipomania was a kind of psychological epidemic, and this is what we believe, the probability exists—bordering on certainty—that one day it will afflict us again in this or another form.

In some Far Eastern port it is getting ready for the journey.

GERARD TERBORCH
The Discreet Charm of the Bourgeoisie

❑

I AM sending you a human figure for your studies to become a painter. It has no pedestal because it was too heavy and too large to fit in the chest; you can have one made for a small sum of money. Use this figure, don't allow it to stand idle as it was here but draw assiduously, especially those large, animated human groups for which Pieter Molyn liked your work so much. If you paint, paint contemporary things, scenes from life, they can be done the most quickly. Be tenacious so you complete the paintings you have started; you will be loved for them, with God's help, just as you were loved in Haarlem and Amsterdam. Whatever you start in the Lord's name will always bring you luck. Serve God above all, be modest and polite toward every man, in this way you will assure your success. I am enclosing also clothes, long brushes, paper, chalk, and all the beautiful paints . . .

This letter, in which elevated and everyday matters mix so naturally, moral teachings as well as painter's accessories, was written in 1635 by Terborch the father from the small town of Zwolle to his seventeen-year-old son Gerard, who was staying at the time in London. Among the sparse, gray materials for biographies of Dutch artists, this is an exceptional document: it preserves the warmth and the glow of a sunny day.

If we may use two old-fashioned expressions in one sentence, we would say he was born under a lucky star and was a child wonder in addition. Well-to-do, his career had no heavy blows, dramas, or crises. His talent developed very early: the preserved drawings of the eight-year-old boy are not only amazingly mature but show the discovery of his own artistic form, his own style. He learned the profession with his father, who was an able draftsman, then with Pieter de Molyn mentioned in the letter. He was seventeen years old when he became a qualified painter included among members of the guild.

In the usual course of events such a promising young artist would now settle down, open an atelier, take in disciples, and begin a family. Terborch junior traveled. His years of wandering were extensive: England, Italy, Spain (where apparently he painted the portrait of Philip IV), France, Flanders, and Germany. He was almost forty years old when after mature reflection he married, settled in the small northern town of Deventer, far from the artistic centers, amid the harmonious clan of Terborchs who bestowed on him their respect and love. He was not only a well-known painter, but what is more important also held the post of City Councillor.

The peak event of his artistic career was a trip to Muenster together with a Dutch delegation conducting peace negotiations with Spain. These were concluded with the signing of a treaty in 1648 that ended eighty years of struggle. It is difficult to overestimate the importance of this event. Terborch recorded the ceremonial moment of the treaty oath.

It is a very peculiar work. Painted on tin, with the dimensions 45 by 58 centimeters, the artist crowded onto this small surface fifty or even as some scholarly sources claim seventy figures of secretaries, high officials, plenipotentiaries and diplomats, not forgetting himself. The whole gives the impression of a rather monotonous, frozen, posed group of people, and the painter, realizing this, tried to breathe life into it by showing some faces in profile and others *en face,* as well as several hands timidly stretched out in the gesture of an oath. The work is not very attractive coloristically: on the left side of the painting a man in a bright red cape, on the right side a young man like an insect, dressed in the golden scales of a sumptuous costume. In the middle, a table covered by fabric that is green verging on black, and on top of it the vermilion cover of a Bible. A lazy light with no luster falls through the window. The painting always makes the impression on me of a ceremony opening a World Congress of Insects. I think I could define some of the species.

I realize I am allowing myself to write blasphemies, because "Swearing of the Oath of Ratification of the Treaty of Muenster," according to general opinion, is a masterpiece. Critics have even seen in the faces of the diplomats (not larger than a fingernail) the struggle of contradictory feelings, fear and hope, joy and depression. I think only that this is not Terborch's best painting, but a very characteristic example of the particularity of Dutch painting. Every pupil of Rubens, Velazquez, or the Italians would set this scene in motion by filling it with noise, color, pathos, hyperbole (because everything has to be made bigger and more splendid), and fill the empty spots under the ceiling with antique gods or archangels blowing their trumpets. Terborch paints his historical work without pathos, in a neutral way as if it were a genre scene that could be imagined more easily on the walls of a middle-class room with a fireplace than in a gala room of a city hall. It is a painting-record, and now we know how it really was. Only in one domain did the painter turn out to be a fantast of unbridled imagination—namely, he requested such a horrendous price for the work that until the end of his life he could not find a buyer.

It seems that for some time Terborch nourished the illusion that he was able to paint lucrative group portraits. Soon after "Swearing of the Oath" he painted "Family against a Landscape"; this picture causes a sudden influx of warm humor, and recalls a canvas painted three centuries later, the "Artillerymen" of the Douanier Rousseau. The mustached soldiers pose as if for a souvenir picture, looking alike as two drops of water, as two buttons of a uniform. Behind them an extremely long cannon barrel seems cast not in metal but heavy dream. In Terborch a group of old men, adults, young people, and children emerges black and foreign, stiff, festive as a colony of mushrooms from the juicy greenness of a ravine.

When I look at Terborch's paintings the impression never leaves me that they are the works of two harmoniously collaborating brothers, a painter and a miniaturist. The silhouettes of the figures emerging from darkness are invariably precise. The strokes of the brush are short, the hand's motion restrained, slow, delicate, without effusion or blurred contours; an attempt to tell the world in a black, pearl-like, and gray tonality.

Terborch stayed in Muenster three long years, and during this time executed a number of portrait studies getting ready, so he thought, for his *magnum opus*. Not many of these sketches and studies remain—so much the more surprising are two excellent miniatures, as if a few measures of an overture moved an entire laboriously composed opera into the shadow.

The first is a portrait of a Spanish aristocrat, at the head of the delegation to the peace negotiations, who carried the sonorous name Don Caspar de Bramante y Guzman Conde de Peneranda. Terborch became so attached to the Spanish diplomat that he placed himself on the side of the "eternal enemies" of his country in the scene of "Swearing of the Oath," and his colleagues pointed out his tactlessness. But the portrait of Conde de Peneranda is excellent. It seems as if the waves of changing moods run through his face: melancholy and serenity, disappointment and tides of energy. A splendid high forehead, sharp pitch-black eyes, and a long, thin, narrow nose like the beak of a sad parrot. A small close-cropped beard, a mustache turned up by a barber's artifice like two sharp hooks. On his neck, like the swish of a sword, a thin cambric collar with the sharp points called *gollilla*. He is dressed in ceremonious court costume, a cape embroidered with gold. Rarely does Terborch give such proof of coloristic virtuosity: dark violet, gold, intensive red juxtaposed against gray and black.

The miniature portrait of the youngest member of the Dutch delegation, Kaspar van Kinschot, is of an entirely different character. He is dressed in a light coat with pale blue and white stripes. His girlish face is encircled by thick hair falling to the shoulders, his big eyes are full of gentle resignation. Poor Kaspar died soon after the signing of the treaty, plunging his native palestra in sorrow as well as the muses, for he was the author of fairly deft Latin poems.

Terborch entered art history as a painter of genre themes and a portraitist. He practiced portrait painting with success, most likely owing much to contacts made in Muenster; the numerous trips from quiet Deventer to Amsterdam, The Hague, Haarlem, and other cities are proof of this. Near the end of his life he received from Prince Cosimo de' Medici III a prestigious order for a life-sized self-portrait with one of his favorite paintings in his hand. Cosimo wanted to create a whole gallery of similar works, "a painting within a painting." Other painters were invited, such as Dou and Mieris, who were popular in France and Italy, and they executed the order quickly. Terborch, on the other hand, delayed, was fussy, grumbled, and wrote that the sum of 500 guldens was decidedly too low. He needed at least four months to execute the "portrait with a picture," putting aside other urgent orders, he was now very busy, and so on. No contemporary painters and few of their descendants possessed to such a degree a business acumen based on two firm principles: never to go below the honorarium designated by the painter, and to value yourself highly in order to be valued by others.

Terborch was an unsurpassed painter of children (his house swarmed with models). The majority of artists painted children as chubby cherubs, or dolls clothed in costumes modeled on those of adults, creatures deprived of their own life and personality—chrysalises looking at us with idiotic expression, or larvae, unfinished dwarfish forms of the human species.

Look at "The Lesson," a painting in the Louvre: a bent head of a boy with thick red hair falling on his forehead like a fur cap emerges from a dark background. We do not see either books or school supplies, yet we know that this silent, concentrated boy is studying the secrets of arithmetic. His mother, seen in profile and indifferent to her son's efforts, looks into the distance as if she wanted to guess his future fate. I have invented all this unnecessary anecdote to motivate these two heads against the heavy, dark background—heads that have nothing in common either from the painterly or compositional point of view.

The "Boy Cleaning His Dog's Coat" in Munich's Old Pinakotheka: a corner of a room, next to the wall a small table with books and school materials, parallel to the lower frame of the painting a bench (Terborch acknowledged only closed, delimited spaces), on the bench an old hat with a large brim. In the middle of this modest scenery a boy sitting on a low stool with a dog on his knees. His agile fingers move along the skin of the animal. The boy applies himself to this activity with tense concentration, with the exclusiveness and total application only children are capable of. Those who "read paintings" cannot agree whether it is in praise of cleanliness or a reproach for preferring unimportant activities to school duties. (Here is an example of the intellectual games of bored elderly gentlemen.) What enchanted me always in this painting were its gentle, noble colors: the toned-down olive-green of the walls, the ochre of the objects, and only two more lively accents, the blue pants of the boy, and the dog's brown and white fur.

Whenever I am in Amsterdam I visit and spend a few moments chatting with Helen van Shalke, a resolute three-year-old girl with dark eyes and small, very red lips. She is in a white dress, a woman's white bonnet, and a white, flaring, wide skirt down to the ground. A basket trimmed in black hangs on a black ribbon from her right arm, which is bent at the elbow. This very basket, inclining backward, destroys the static perpendicular axis of the composition: whirling movement, restlessness. For indeed Helen appears here only for a moment; she looks at us with curiosity and anxiety, she will immediately run away to her inconceivable childish worlds.

The psychological inquisitiveness of the painter bordered on prophesying the future, because when he painted the twelve-year-old son of Wilhelm III of Orange, Henry Casimir van Nassau Dietz, he represented a young man with a long face and not a single trace of grace, with small drilling eyes and tight lips. Indeed, the prince grew up to be a man of difficult character, to speak delicately.

Terborch created his own type of portrait, fundamentally different from that of Hals, Rembrandt, and other masters of the period, and with his own inimitable style. He strove for an almost extreme reduction of painterly means. He substituted a play of colors with a broad scale of grayness, and built a static, cohesive form. Usually he painted an entire figure standing against a dark wall, dressed in a thick woolen cape loosely falling from the shoulders, a frock coat, trousers down to the knees, pearly gray stockings, and elegant low shoes clasped with a buckle, the right one placed forward and the left arranged perpendicular to the lower frame of the painting, endowing the figures—even those markedly corpulent—with an almost dancelike grace. The entire composition could be compared to a spindle or two cones connected at their bases. On the basis of what was said about him, one might judge that Terborch was an engraver who for some unknown reason used oil paints. When seen from a distance the background of the painting "Portrait of a Man" in the Louvre has a dull tone, *noir d'ivoire.* Looking closer we notice irregular stripes of deep juicy browns. The background becomes differentiated and sonorous.

With few exceptions the persons portrayed by Terborch who face the spectator stand in an empty space without doors, windows, or furniture. Only occasionally an ordinary chair or table appears, and there is only enough light to show faces, hands, and the white accessories of their dress.

Who ordered these unattractive canvases? We know the Dutch loved objects, the worldly reward for industriousness and saving. The ship owner would be portrayed against a window through which all of his ships could be seen. Gabriel Metsu paints a splendid fat man sprawled out in an armchair surrounded by his wife, children, servants, and his paintings hanging on the walls; the open door with a stone portal leads to further splendors. Terborch's clients—regents and patricians—despised such ostentatiousness. They are found in his paintings without the insignia of office, without proofs of affluence. The master painted them delicately but surely standing on the ground, combining the intimate and monumental in these portraits, ease and hieratic posture, the ceremonial and the everyday. This is how they have come down to our days, these very conservative representatives of Calvinist virtues and archetypal accumulation of capital.

Terborch's genre paintings do not overstep the thematic range of Dutch painting—military scenes, mothers combing children, a few persons giving a concert in an elegant interior, a suitor playing an instrument, and a lady—but almost always they contain an element of distance, irony, and discreetly concealed ambiguity. In Kassel, which has a very decent museum, we find Terborch's painting representing a lonely woman playing the lute. Most likely it was Gasina, Gerard's favorite sister and model, an unmarried, talented woman whose rounded forehead and upturned nose we encounter in many of the master's paintings. A duet of a man and a lady signified, as a rule, a prelude to a love game. Then what does this portrait mean—a lonely woman in a white dress and satin doublet with a golden sheen, lined with white fur? In her artfully arranged light hair there are four short vermilion ribbons. The painter caught the moment of indecision, anxiety: she is bent forward with eyes fixed on the musical score as if looking for a lost note or chord in the bushel of other notes. We do not know for whom this lady is playing—is it a lament for someone who has gone, or the lure of a nightingale?

Terborch was a peculiar colorist. He avoided what we call the building of form with color. Muted browns, ochres, and grays prevail in his reticent paintings; against these backgrounds a dress suddenly explodes in shades of ultramarine, luminous yellows, cinnabar red.

The seventeenth century was an epistolary century. The postal service started to function almost as well as in Roman times, many Dutchmen were on the sea or in colonies, the literary culture of the middle class was high; therefore, conditions were favorable for a lively exchange of correspondence. Those who did not know how to express their feelings artfully had different aids at their disposal; a manual, *Le secrétaire à la mode* by Jean Puget de la Serra, appeared in Amsterdam and by the middle of the century had already been through nineteen editions. Characteristic in this manual is the distinct division of roles. Gentlemen were allowed to reveal stormy feelings and an abyss of melancholy; ladies charmed with the soothing depth of lakes.

He: "Since your departure I lead a life sad beyond words. I confess I have lost appetite and peace; I spend entire days without food and nights without sleep." She: "If I could only soothe the suffering caused by my absence you would see me in person instead of this letter. But I remain in the custody of my mother and father, and I don't have enough freedom even to write you." Then words of consolation follow, and a veiled hope of a meeting.

In Dutch painting the theme of the letter was extremely popular. Formally it is simply a portrait, always of a female, a girl or a woman who puts down the letter or else reads from a piece of paper. For us this does not contain anything extraordinary: a simple monodrama played by one actress with a single prop. For the Dutch of the seventeenth century this kind of painting was particularly exciting, because the piece of paper was not, after all, an object emotionally indifferent like a mug or ball of yarn. As a rule, the women represented in these paintings are reading love letters. Thus we are looking at an intimate scene, intruders in a dialogue with an absentee, but we will never learn the reproaches, complaints, or confessions. The words, conceived in solitude, read in silence, are enclosed by the solemn silence of the painting as if with a seal.

Terborch paints "Young Lady Writing a Letter" (in The Hague) against a background of a bed's dark red curtains arranged in the shape of a tent. On the table, disorder—inkstands, a sheaf of papers, a colorful cloth in brick-brown, pearl-gray, and blue patterns hurriedly pushed aside. The girl, shown in profile, is dressed in a jacket that has a lively orange, luminous tinge. Amid the disquiet of the objects and colors, her face does not express any emotion. She recalls, rather, a student scrupulously doing her homework. Similarly, "Lady Reading a Letter" in the Metropolitan Museum is dressed in a deep funereal black, and even in her light hair there is a black lace scarf. She has a beautiful young alabaster face without a shade of sadness, without a wrinkle of worry. She reads the letter (perhaps an offer of marriage, since widows were highly valued on the Dutch matrimonial market) with the sober objectivity of a notary.

Sometimes, however, Terborch has pity for our curiosity and sinful habit of peeking. The "Woman Reading" in the London Wallace Collection does not conceal her feelings. All-absorbed in reading a letter, she smiles at the piece of paper held in her hand, which emanates warmth and light. Her face is blissful, as if she found in the letter all the long-expected words and entreaties. In the Old Pinakothek in Munich there is a painting by Terborch that has the content of the letter written out for different voices: a military courier enters the room dressed in a long brown coat decorated with black stripes—a beautiful Braque-like juxtaposition—and a trumpet on his shoulder, a lady with a white bonnet on her head is clearly interrupted in her morning toilet, and in addition a servant girl looks at the scene with indescribable amazement. The courier holds a letter in his outstretched hand; the mistress's face expresses a spiteful coldness, and she has crossed her hands on her chest in a pathetic gesture signifying rejection, a rebuff, and a final break in the relationship. It would move one to tears if the toilette were not in the way: it is difficult to play a heroine in morning attire, or Penelope in pajamas.

The "Fatherly Admonition" in Berlin's Dahlem Museum is my favorite Terborch, one might say the fullest Terborch at the peak of his painterly potentiality: the enclosed fragment of an elegant room (its box conception of space brings to mind the dramas of Ibsen and nineteenth-century naturalists). Against deep browns the screen of a bed with a baldachin and a curtain falling perpendicularly like a backdrop with a matte red shade. The same color, only gradually more intensive and saturated with light, is repeated in the coverlet on the table and upholstery of a chair. Three persons are in the room. A young soldier seen in profile, his leather jacket and trousers painted with light warm ochre; in the left hand on his knee he holds a hat decked with fantastic feathers, in the right hand lifted to his face the thumb and index finger touch, as if he wanted to stress with this gesture the importance and subtlety of the spoken words. A woman in black faces the spectator, her eyes drowned in a glass of wine. And finally, her—the heroine of the painting, with her back turned to us, haughty, slender, precious. Terborch dressed her in a lordly manner. Her blond hair, combed up and gathered in a black ribbon, reveals a beautiful neck, a black, wide, velvet shawl-like collar, puffed sleeves, a dress with a high waist and silvery undulating satin that flows down from the waist, forming a small train on the floor. Terborch, who painted with such reticence gray and black portraits, gives in "Fatherly Admonition" a concert of coloristic mastery in difficult chromatic compositions: red, black, matte white, the subdued red of the bed curtain, the low deadly black of the model's collar, and the light, dazzling, joyful white of her dress. Whenever I try to recall this painting of Terborch, I close my eyes and see first of all the heroine of the scene, a "beauty with her back turned" who brightens the darkness like a candle in a precious candlestick, while other persons, objects, details remain unclear, blurred and wavering.

In his novel *Wahlverwandschaften*, Goethe describes a popular game of the time in which a tableau was acted out. A work of art was reconstructed as faithfully as possible by persons in appropriate costumes; they imitated the gestures, expressions, and atmosphere of the original. In a word: painting transposed for the stage of a theater, frozen in immobility and silence.

One evening they performed Van Dyke's "Belissarius," Poussin's "Ashuarus and Esther," and then Terborch's "Fatherly Admonition." Precisely this painting provoked the unusual enthusiasm of the spectators, thunderous applause, and calls of "encore." It was the figure of "the girl with her back turned" that won their hearts most of all, her artfully arranged hair, the shape of her head, her lightness. One of the enchanted spectators called out, "Tournez, s'il vous plaît," others joined in, but the artists who knew the rules of the game remained indifferent and unmoved.

A few centuries passed during which a dispute, even a scandal, broke out about the interpretation of "Fatherly Admonition." Those who "read paintings" announced that the title had been invented by bigots and in fact the painting represented—fearful to admit—a scene from a public house. Dutch painters often composed the interiors of brothels with tipsy men and concubines pouring wine, intently staring at the purses of their clients (not to leave any doubts, they would also add copulating dogs). However Terborch did everything to mislead us. The interior in "Fatherly Admonition" is really the interior of a well-to-do bourgeois home. The whole scene is steeped in an atmosphere of honesty, peacefulness, and reticence. Not a trace of violent gestures or unbridled lust. Such is the general impression. Inexorable realities indicate something different. Could a young soldier in his twenties be the father of "the beauty with her back turned"? Why has the golden coin that he temptingly holds in his right hand been erased (traces of retouching are visible on the canvas)? Is the woman in black sipping wine a mother, or simply a procuress—paintings with similar subjects show them—an intermediary in a sinful relationship? In emblematics all this game of meanings in which Terborch delighted is called a paradox; it consists in showing a morally reprehensible event with irreproachable decorations, saturated with virtue and nobility.

Compared to the boring, obsessively "scientific" studies of contemporary scholars, dry as sawdust, how favorably the old art historians' manner of writing stands out: a flowing style not without charm, always appealing to our ability to see, always hitting the mark with short, synthetic silhouettes of the masters under consideration. The incomparable Max Friedländer characterizes Terborch in the following way: "Good taste, tact, and sense of proportion inform his work. He endowed the Dutch bourgeoisie with a touch of French grace and Spanish *grandezza,* and it seems he possesses all the traits of a diplomat: elegance full of dignity, and a reserved spirit of conciliation." The subtle drawing of Terborch, his avoiding of violent coloristic compositions, the cool, silvery tonality and gradations of gray all the way to the majestic black that encloses the painting, do not escape Friedländer's attention. Also Terborch's mastery in rendering the consistency of objects, especially fabrics, from rustling cool silks to meaty wool that absorbs light. Finally, the peculiar eroticism of the artist: puritanical, coded, barely mentioned but so much the more intriguing.

Indeed Terborch gives the impression of an artist who is one of a kind, without genealogy, influences, or evolution—therefore easily recognizable. But is this really so? At least two of his paintings do not give me peace. The first is the "Grinder's Family" in Berlin's Dahlem.

At the rear of a courtyard, a murky shed patched together with boards—the atelier of an artisan who at this moment bends over his wheel waiting for a client. On the right, something that once might have been a house but has been reduced by time to one floor made of bricks, with peeling stucco. Three dark openings imitate windows and a door. A mother who is delousing a child, a courtyard paved with cobbles, an overturned chair, tools in disarray. The whole is a study of abandonment, dilapidation, and poverty. With what obstinate precision this painter of elegance and synthesis traces all the repelling details and horrible minutiae. The naturalists of the middle of the nineteenth century painted this way trying to evoke compassion for the fate of the urban proletariat. But how did the elegant Councillor Terborch hit upon this alley-way of misery?

The "Procession of Flagellants" from the Rotterdam Museum Boymans van Beuningen I took without hesitation to be an error of an absentminded curator who hung a Spaniard among the Dutch. The "Procession" is a scene of violent, sharp contrasts of chiaroscuro. The atmosphere of menace and mysteriousness oscillates between a rending shout and deadly silence. Light falls from the lit torches, creating puddles of brightness amid thick, almost fleshlike darkness. On the left, something like an altar or a tribune. In the center, three exorcists in white frocks and white conical hoods recall predatory animals in an atlas of nightmarish hallucinations. We also see a man tied to a fence or wall with stretched-out arms, bare to his waist, on whom a storm of whiplashes will fall in a moment.

When later I looked at this painting, many times I invariably thought: But this is Goya, no one else but Goya—his subject matter, his way of painting, his violence and cruelty. How can it be that a painter from a northern country, where other tastes and traditions govern art, has anticipated by a century and a half the great Spaniard? A memory from Terborch's youthful travels? Very likely, but this does not explain the similarities or identity of style. A lesson in humility. We will never solve all the secrets of the imagination.

In the Mauritshius, a self-portrait of the master: a large head somewhat out of proportion with the rest of the body, a rather common face, thick nose, gluttonous lips, and sharp eyes looking at us with unconcealed irony, as if he were saying, Yes I knew well the world of poverty and ugliness, but I painted the skin, the glittering surface, the appearance of things: the silky ladies, and gentlemen in irreproachable black. I admired how fiercely they fought for a life slightly longer than the one for which they were destined. They protected themselves with fashion, tailors' accessories, a fancy ruffle, ingenious cuffs, a fold, a pleat, any detail that would allow them to last a little longer before they—and we as well—are engulfed by the black background.

STILL LIFE
WITH A BRIDLE

❏

For Jozef Czapski
Car je est un autre
(ARTHUR RIMBAUD)

1.

THIS is how it happened. Years ago, during my first visit to the Royal Museum in Amsterdam, I was crossing a room with the marvelous "Married Couple" of Hals and the beautiful "Concert" of Duyster when I came upon a canvas by a painter unknown to me.

I understood immediately, though it is hard to explain rationally, something very important had happened; something far more important than an accidental encounter in a crowd of masterpieces. How to describe this inner state? A suddenly awakened intense curiosity, sharp concentration with the senses alarmed, hope for an adventure and consent to be dazzled. I experienced an almost physical sensation as if someone called me, summoned me. The painting registered for long years in my memory, sharply etched and insistent, but it was not an image of a face with fiery eyes or even a dramatic scene, but a calm, static still life.

Here is an inventory of the objects represented in the painting: on the left side a potbellied pitcher of burnt clay in a warm, saturated brown; in the middle a massive glass goblet, called a *romer*, half-filled with liquid; and on the right side a silver-gray pewter pitcher with a lid and spout. In addition two porcelain pipes, a piece of paper with music, and a text on the shelf where the utensils were standing. At the top, metal objects I could not at first identify.

The background was the most fascinating of all: black, deep as a precipice and at the same time flat as a mirror, palpable and disappearing in perspectives of infinity. A transparent cover over the abyss.

At the time I jotted down the name of the painter, Torrentius. Then I looked for more information about him in various art histories, encyclopedias, and dictionaries of artists. But the dictionaries and encyclopedias were silent, or I found only confused and deceptive references. It seemed Torrentius was a hypothesis of scholars, but in fact never existed.

When I finally went to the original sources and documents, the amazing life of the painter suddenly appeared before my eyes—an unusual, dramatic, stormy life completely different from the banal biographies of most of his professional colleagues. For the few who wrote about him he was an enigmatic, disquieting figure. His glittering career and tragic end did not form any logical or clear pattern, but made an entangled knot of many threads—artistic, social, moral, and finally, it seems, political.

In good bourgeois fashion his name was simply Jan Simon van de Beeck. His Latin nom de guerre comes from the word *torrens*, which in its adjectival form means "hot, incandescent," and as a noun means "a wild, rushing stream"—the two unreconciled, antagonistic elements of fire and water. If one could write one's own destiny into a pen name, Torrentius did it with prophetic intuition.

He was born in Amsterdam in 1589. We do not know who his master was, but we know that from the beginning of his artistic career Torrentius was a famous, fashionable, and wealthy painter. His still lifes in particular enjoyed tremendous success. "In my opinion," Constantine Huyghens wrote in his *Observations on Painting*, "he is a magician in representing still objects."

The Orpheus of the still life. He was surrounded by an aura of mystery, and legends circulated about what took place in his atelier, tales about supernatural forces he brought into his work. Probably Torrentius thought a certain dose of charlatanism did not harm art (differing here from his modest guild brothers of the Fraternity of Saint Luke), but on the contrary helped it. For example, he used to say he did not in fact paint but only placed paints on the floor next to his canvases; under the influence of musical sounds they arranged themselves in colorful harmonies. But is not art, every art, a kind of alchemical transmutation? From pigments dissolved in oil arise flowers, towns, bays of the ocean, and views of paradise truer than the real ones.

"As for the life and conduct of that man," Huyghens adds as if in passing, "I would not want to assume the role of a Roman judge in a toga." Discretion worthy of praise, because it was just this subject that was much discussed, universally and with fierce relish. Torrentius was handsome, dressed with sophisticated elegance, led a magnificent life, had a lackey, and rode a horse. What is worse, he surrounded himself with a group of friends and admirers, wandering from town to town with them like Dionysus leading a crowd of satyrs, organizing sumptuous, not-quite-decent feasts in taverns, inns, and public houses. The notoriety of a scandalizer and libertine followed him; the claims and grievances of seduced women increased as well as his unpaid bills. In the Leyden tavern Under the Rainbow alone, his debt for food and drink amounted to the not trivial sum of 484 florins. Some gently called him an epicurean, others did not spare stern words of condemnation: *in summa seductor civium, impostor populi, corruptor juventutis, stupator feminarum.*

If all this was not enough, Torrentius had a Socratic streak, namely a predilection for discussions on the subject of faith. He was intelligent, well-read, brilliant, and missed no opportunity to get the better of a pastor or theology student. It is hard to say what religious views he represented. Most likely his disputes were only displays of dialectics, and their motive was the pure pleasure in making fools out of others.

Torrentius must have realized he was playing with fire, and pursued a dangerous game. But he counted on his lucky star, his talent, and his irresistible personal charm. The role he first assumed, lightheartedly and for show, became part of his self, and began to direct his destiny.

Dark clouds began to gather over the painter's head, and they took on quite unexpected shapes. A suspicion arose that he was a member and even leader of the Dutch secret association of Rosicrucians (a kind of freemasonry *avant la lettre*), whose goal was mystical reform, renewal of the world, and preparation for a divine kingdom on earth. Different elements united in the philosophy, or what they called Pan-sophy or Omni-wisdom, of this movement: the Kaballa, Neo-Platonism, Gnosis, the esoteric interpretation of Christianity, and most of all the views of the German theologian Johann Valentine Andreae. At the end of the sixteenth century and later the Rosicrucians had a sizable number of adepts, particularly in England, France, and Germany. Among them were many distinguished personalities of the time, princes, scholars, and thinkers. Indeed it was a very appealing current, since it attracted fine minds like Komensky, Leibniz, and Descartes.

Secret associations do not leave a register of their members for posterity, therefore it is hard to ascertain whether Torrentius was a Rosicrucian. But it is a fact that surveillance of the painter started for this reason. The Republic's authorities might have been afraid of the activities of this secret confraternity, with its far-flung international influence; in 1625 an agreement between French and Dutch Rosicrucians was discovered in Haarlem. But this might just as well have been a pretext. Holland was famous for religious and denominational liberty, unparalleled elsewhere in Europe. The following event best illustrates the spiritual situation in the homeland of Erasmus.

In 1596 an artisan accused of heresy was brought before a tribunal in Amsterdam. He was a cobbler by profession, but an unusual one because he had learned Latin and Hebrew by himself to study the Bible. During these studies, carried out with the proverbial passion of cobblers, he came to the conclusion that Christ was only a man. He talked about it widely with his relatives and friends, and, what is worse, with strangers. The accusation of heresy could theoretically lead to the stake, but one of the mayors of Amsterdam intervened in the trial and took up the defense of the unfortunate enthusiast of the Bible, proving that if the Church had already dispensed appropriate spiritual punishment—exclusion from the community of the faithful—it was unnecessary for fallible human justice to pronounce a verdict once again in this intricate matter. He also said that human life should not depend on the subtle considerations of theologians.

Quite unexpectedly, on June 30, 1627, Torrentius was arrested and put in prison in Haarlem.

In the beginning one could suppose the whole affair would end quietly, primo, with a paternal reprimand from the tribunal; secundo, with an earnest promise by the repentant sinner to desist; and tertio, with a heavy fine. It soon appeared, however, that the matter was taking a fatal turn, and that even before probate proceedings the court was trying to sentence the criminal artist at any price, severely and using any pretext.

This was shown by the huge number of witnesses who were called. Personal enemies of Torrentius were predominant, and these were innumerable. Testimonies concerned the two kinds of offense the painter was accused of: breaking obligatory moral norms, and impiety. With regard to the first, abundant criminal evidence was provided for the court by servants from the houses in which the artist lived, owners of taverns, and accidental witnesses of his notorious extravaganzas.

One of them saw this intimate scene: Torrentius with a young woman on his lap. Another, the owner of the tavern Under the Snake, in Delft, told a moving story about a girl to whom the painter threw candies through a window until she succumbed to him, and when she became pregnant he viciously abandoned her. In addition, he publicly laughed at her. A member of the well-known family van Beresteyn also came forward as witness; he asserted that Torrentius brought women of easy virtue together in a tavern, using a letter from the Prince of Orange, *salvia guardia,* as his authority. Supposedly it gave him power over the demimonde of the entire Republic. Van Beresteyn also testified that the accused organized feasts for honorable councillors and wealthy merchants, inviting young ladies from honest households; these were followed by collective carnal pleasures. One might prolong the list of accusations; most likely truth was mixed with gossip, honest testimony with vile denunciations. But let us stop with these selected examples. It seems more important to attempt to answer the question of whether Torrentius, against the background of the manners of his time, was a figure impossible to accept: a malicious type of moral monster.

The English ambassador William Temple, a keen observer of the life of the Dutch, says their temperament and traits of character were conditioned by their physical constitution; reasonable and moderate by nature, they did not succumb to great passions, of course with some exceptions. The severity of Calvinism in the Republic was tempered by a universal spirit of tolerance. A sizable margin of freedom existed next to exemplary bourgeois and philistine morality. Someone rightly observed that the liberty so beloved by the Dutch originated in hatred of force rather than the fascination with abstract slogans, in which various revolutionaries did, and do, excel. Imposing achievements in the domain of democracy were guarded to a greater degree by custom, to a smaller degree by institutions. Likewise, tolerance usually ended when it encountered extremes, for example blatant manifestations of disbelief. In 1642 Francis van den Meurs, who did not believe in the divinity of Christ and the immortality of the soul, was put in the Amsterdam prison. He stayed there seven months, then was released.

Morality was severe, especially in the villages. Choice of future wives and betrothals were regulated by rules of century-old traditions and, just in case, took place under the watchful eyes of grown-ups. Of course the young preferred less formal ways of meeting: on the ice rink, in secluded places in the woods, on the shore of the sea, even in church. The pastors thundered against this from their pulpits, meddling in every possible and impossible matter of daily life. They fought against the theater, tobacco smoking, drinking coffee, pompous funerals, lavish weddings; they condemned long hair for men, silver platters, and even Sunday excursions outside town. The faithful listened with pious expressions and did what they pleased. Marriage was in general a solid institution. A father or husband had the right to punish a woman caught in *flagrante;* in such cases, even murder could go unpunished. They shut their eyes when a single man maintained relations with an unmarried woman, provided he kept up necessary appearances; but if he was married and caught in the midst of sinful, amorous cooing, he usually paid a hefty fine.

In comparison with most European royal and aristocratic courts of the time, the court of the sovereigns of the Netherlands was an oasis of modesty. Only William II spoiled this exemplary image of moderation and virtue. His exuberant temperament was a charming subject for biting satires and ephemeral poems, while his all-too-numerous love affairs were pointed out even on theater stages.

On the other hand, a widespread, half-pagan institution existed that was deeply rooted in tradition, namely, fairs—a combination of market, church holiday, and an explosion of unbridled folk licence. Hundreds of paintings represent these Dutch bacchanalia (it is impossible to understand the life of the Dutch without them). A crowd of parsimonious peasants and artisans undergoes a sudden metamorphosis; they hang their steadfast virtues on a peg and gladly succumb to the temptations of the Seven Capital Sins. The aftermath of these fairs was a huge number of children born out of wedlock, and foundlings. Patient public benevolence built ever new houses and orphanages for them.

In the big cities and especially the ports, prostitution thrived. No attempts were even made to fight it, as people realized the effort was in vain, yet the sense of order required these social phenomena to be contained within certain limits. It was done in an original way. In some districts of Amsterdam the care of the houses of ill-fame was entrusted to policemen, and these guardians of public order collaborated with prostitutes in exemplary harmony. They carried out a procedure not quite legal but lucrative. The streetwalker, disguised as a young girl, lured an honest, rich citizen to a specific spot where the police were already waiting and meted out to the "seducer" an appropriate monetary fine. Most likely everyone paid, fearing a scandal.

How did the "Torrentius case" look against this background? To speak delicately, the painter violated generally accepted moral norms; he did it systematically, from conviction, and ostentatiously as a confession of faith. Therefore the artist's main guilt was not his exuberant and dissolute life but the atmosphere of scandal and notoriety he gave to his vagaries. Bourgeois morality does not excuse this. The collected evidence of his guilt in the matter did not yet constitute a basis for imposing a stiff penalty. So a charge of a much greater weight was drawn up: namely, impiety.

It is well known that this is not a precise concept and leaves a wide field for legal interpreters to display their talents. The privilege of lack of clarity has only too often been abused in history, usually with fatal consequences for the accused. In the case of Torrentius, they wanted to prove that the painter was an avowed, aggressive blasphemer who fought not only the dogmas of faith but doubted the existence of God.

Then it began, *horribile dictu* because the affair took place in enlightened Holland. Testimonies were collected to prove a close connection between the painter and the unclean powers. Someone informed that Torrentius often strolled in the forest, where he had conversations with the devil, far from human eyes; that he bought a black rooster and a hen at the market for his supposedly magical practices; and that voices of immaterial beings came from his atelier. It is easy to guess that these were whispers of completely corporeal ladies who visited the painter under cover of darkness.

Accommodating owners of taverns and inns where Torrentius used to spend rollicking evenings and nights outdid one another in providing proofs of his guilt. What kind of proofs? To say the least, dubious proofs: overheard conversations, bits of dialogue, even drunken shouts. They did not form any logical whole. So much the better.

One witness testified that the painter pronounced incomprehensible remarks about the Trinity and Christ's Passion,

86

others informed that Torrentius once called the Bible a muzzle put on enlightened minds, he thought the Deluge too severe a punishment against humanity, he had his own views on the subject of hell and paradise, once a toast to Satan was drunk in his presence, he also addressed women by using his favorite expression, "My soul desires your body."

The court did not want to acknowledge the simple fact that the painter was talkative by nature; when excited by wine and joyous company demanding displays of extravagance, he provoked, scandalized, spouted nonsense—in a word, entertained his companions and not always in the best style. What is worse, voices raised in favor of the accused were not taken into consideration. A young painter from Delft, Christian van Couwenberch, and his father testified under oath that during their six-year acquaintance with Torrentius they did not hear a single blasphemy from his mouth. On the contrary, he always defended the truth of the faith with zeal, and he also attacked Socinians and other heretics. The court annotated this kind of testimony with the comment "nihil," which means it was rejected without any reasons given.

Torrentius was alone. All the legal guarantees of the accused were waived, because extraordinary proceedings were ordered that did not even permit a defense. The indictment accused him with thirty-one counts; the most severe concerned heresy and offense against what is sacred.

He was interrogated five times, the last on December 29, 1627, in extraordinary circumstances, about which more in a moment. Torrentius defended himself with consistency, logic, and persuasion, realizing it was a game for high stakes. Yes, it is true he often took advantage of the services of different girls, but as a painter of mythological scenes (a rare genre in Holland) he always looked for models ready to pose naked, because the Olympians had a liking for this.

When he organized feasts in some setting of not the best reputation, he invited exclusively adult males, who realized that they were not coming to meditate on riddles of existence. Therefore, he was not a depraver in the ordinary sense of the word.

Energetically and deliberately he refuted the accusations about questions of religion: he never insulted God or attacked dogma. Yes, it happened that he discussed religious subjects with passion and the inquisitiveness born of a restless conscience, but even this testified to his advantage, because it showed these problems were important for him. Other citizens behaved the same way. A curious thing—during the investigation the accusation that Torrentius belonged to a secret association simply evaporated. Yet it was the point of departure for the whole action.

Against the background of Dutch court chronicles of the seventeenth century, Torrentius's trial is the most convoluted, obscure, and morally repelling, especially from the moment when the decision was taken to employ methods of physical force against the accused. The court, unable to force an admission of guilt from Torrentius, decided to break him by torture. This method belonged to the repertory of the hated Inquisition and continued to be used only for common criminals, yet the accused did not belong to this category in any way. The Haarlem judges certainly realized they had gone too far when they addressed a letter to five eminent jurists from The Hague, asking them for an opinion as to whether such drastic methods of investigation were permitted in this case. The five famous lawyers responded: the application of torture to those who commit a weighty offense against divine majesty is a legal means.

"If something slips from my lips when you inflict suffering on me, it will be a lie," the artist supposedly shouted at his torturers. An amazing thing happened: the tools to force his confession appeared to be powerless. Torrentius did not admit the crimes he was accused of.

On January 28, 1628, a verdict was pronounced: burning at the stake, and hanging of the corpse from a gallows. As if frightened by its own cruelty, the court changed the punishment to twenty years in prison. It was synonymous with slow death in a dungeon.

To the credit of Dutch society it has to be stated that this cruel verdict had wide repercussions and provoked outrage, though of course bigots gave voice to their satisfaction. Many leaflets appeared claiming the whole trial was a return to the practices of the Spanish occupiers. Eminent lawyers protested to the city authorities, claiming that the legal guarantees to which the accused was entitled were systematically violated during the investigation and court proceedings. The prosecutor's office, with a calm undisturbed by pangs of conscience, answered simply that in the case of Torrentius the severity of the crimes committed justified the extraordinary procedure.

Even Holland's regent, Prince Frederick Henry, took a lively interest in the whole matter. He could not have the slightest influence on its outcome, but during the trial he demanded an impartial investigation. After the verdict, he listened to reports by friends of the condemned painter who informed him that Torrentius remained in complete isolation from the world, without medical aid or the possibility of practicing his profession. The prince proposed that the artist be freed from prison. He promised he would give instructions to find another suitable place of isolation where the condemned man would find care, supervision, and the conditions indispensable for creative work.

The fathers of the respected city of Haarlem answered with a letter full of courtesies and subterfuges. They maintained that the condemned man was not as badly off as he was reputed to be. The prison guard took care of him as if he were his servant; the prisoner had a surgeon at his disposal, but he refused to undergo the necessary small surgical interventions (marks of torture could be seen "only" on his legs). His friends brought him linen and delicate food (it was probably their delicate consideration that prevented the councillors from mentioning that intensive interrogations of the prisoner had resulted in a damaged jaw, and problems with eating). No one had objections, either, to his performing his art, but clearly he did not feel like it. Therefore the release of Torrentius from prison, even on the conditions proposed by the prince, seemed neither necessary nor just. Such an unmerited act of clemency would be interpreted by the majority of healthy public opinion as undermining the principles of justice, and it would encourage some toward similarly scandalous crimes. Also, one could not exclude a wave of protests and disturbances, because citizens expect the protection of laws, good manners, and religion from the authorities. Besides, a justified fear existed that even in his place of isolation Torrentius would continue to be what he was until now—that is, a scandalizer and blasphemer.

The only positive result of the intervention of the regent was that the prison regime was made less severe. More frequent visits by the painter's friends were allowed, his wife could spend fourteen days in his cell, every day he was permitted to buy a pitcher of wine exempt from the city tax—O what magnanimity—also a special commission of experts was convened, headed by Frans Hals, to examine whether one could perform art under prison conditions. It is deplorable that the report on this important and, unfortunately, still contemporary question has not survived to our times.

Everything indicated that Torrentius's fate was sealed, that he would never see the light of freedom.

But suddenly matters took an unexpected turn, expanding

in an amazingly wide circle. For behold, the Prince of Orange received a letter from the King of England, Charles I. The document is dated May 30, 1630:

"Mon cousin"—wrote the English monarch—"having learned that a certain Torrentius, painter by profession, has been confined for several years in the municipal prison of Haarlem by virtue of a verdict decreed against him for scandalous behavior and profanation of religion, we want to assure you it is not our intention to undermine the justness of the aforementioned verdict nor to request that the punishment be shortened or alleviated because as we believe it justly fell upon him for such great crimes . . . ." Here ends a convoluted introduction intended to dispel any suspicion that the king might intervene "in internal Dutch affairs," and we reach the conclusion. Charles I asks that out of consideration for his great talent, Torrentius be released and sent to England *"près de nous"*—that is, to the court. There he will devote himself entirely to painting, and attentive eyes will watch that he does not fall into his old habits and inclinations.

One might succumb to the pleasant illusion that these words flowed from the tender heart of a monarch moved by the cruel fate of an artist. What is more probable is that Charles I—a well-known art lover, whose court painter, after all, was Van Dyke himself—decided simply to take advantage of the situation and procure the famous Torrentius cheaply, in exchange for an unclear promise of royal favors. One way or another diplomatic machinery was set in motion. The Secretary of State Viscount Dorchester intervened with Holland's Pensionary de Glarges; the royal ambassador Sir Dudley Carleton was particularly active in the affair. In nearly all letters the same argument is repeated: it would be a great loss if such an eminent artist miserably passed away.

These efforts were crowned with success. Torrentius left

91

prison, but under three conditions: he had to pay the high costs of the trial, solemnly promise that he would leave for England immediately, and never return to his homeland.

We can re-create the further fate of the painter only in very general outline. Nothing certain is known about his stay in England. It seems that in the land of his saviors the incorrigible Torrentius continued his old lifestyle. This at least is how one can interpret an enigmatic mention of him, "giving more scandal than satisfaction," that we find in Horace Walpole's book *Painters in the Reign of Charles I.*

His return to Holland clearly borders on madness. He suddenly appeared in 1642, and indeed it is impossible to say what he counted on. That his guilt would be forgiven, and the biblical story of the Prodigal Son be repeated? After all, he knew the unrelenting hatred of Haarlem's bourgeois only too well. Maybe the exile was simply forced to flee from his place of asylum, and he could do nothing but return to his homeland, hoping with work to earn better memory from future generations. It is quite possible Torrentius also wanted to challenge fate to a last duel, find his old companions and experience with them a few wild nights, recalling his youth with a Faustian gesture regardless of the price to be paid. Finally, it is not out of the question that he felt deadly tired of a game he himself had invented, and did not care what the continuation and finale might be of this tale full of sound and fury.

He met what everyone could have easily predicted—a second trial, of which hardly anything is known except that once again he underwent tortures. He died in his native Amsterdam a broken man on February 14, 1644.

The fate of Torrentius brings to mind a novel. But what kind? An adventure novel, or allegory? Our hero escapes formulas, definitions, and traditional descriptions, as if his only ambition after death was to deceive and repeat that he was a guest from nowhere, without ancestors, progeny, or relatives, an inhabitant of infinity.

It would be a modest statement, coming barely half a step closer to Torrentius's mystery, if we were to say that he was different, not at all like the other citizens of the Republic, a provocatively colorful bird amid birds of a uniform color. He probably treated his own life like a material substance to which he gave unusually sophisticated form; therefore he destroyed conventions, bewildered, and scandalized.

He deserves the title and sad dignity of precursor, for there was something of the Marquis de Sade in him, and something of the nineteenth-century *poètes maudits*, or to use a closer analogy, the Surrealists. He was ahead of his times, as if demanding the exceptional status of an artist in exchange for unusual works, and this was completely beyond the comprehension of the upright bourgeois, bourgeois painters included. This is why Torrentius had to suffer a defeat.

For us he remains the creator of a single painting, and a curious case on the borderline of politics, the history of manners, and art.

What happened to his works? It is justified to fear they shared the fate of their author and were destroyed. But here and there one comes upon their traces, in inventories and brief references by contemporaries. Kramm, who wrote in the first half of the seventeenth century, mentions the portrait of a theologian. The painting was composed of two mobile surfaces, one placed on top of the other. The first represented the honorable scholar of divine affairs; when it was moved, before astonished eyes would appear "an artistic, unusually well-done scene from a public house." Not bad.

In the inventory of the collection of Charles I we find a notation about three paintings by Torrentius, terse but thought-provoking: "One is an Adam and Eve, his flesshe very ruddy, theye show there syde faces. The other is a woman

93

pissing in a mans eare. The best of those 3 is a young woman sitting somewhat odly with her hand under her legg."

Many works of art have been condemned to a secret life, and what we see in the museums and art galleries, accessible to everyone, is only a part of the existing heritage of the past. The impenetrable remainder winters in closed labyrinths, treasure houses, and hiding places together with valuable papers jealously guarded by not always enlightened collectors. Therefore it is not out of the question—though the chances are not great—that a new Torrentius will emerge one day.

At a Parisian auction in 1865 a canvas by our painter was sold. No doubt it was signed, since at that time he was in the limbo of forgetfulness. We only know the title, "Diana and Actaeon." Neither a reproduction nor even a description of the work has been preserved. The situation was changed radically, as if touched by a wand (the object of our investigation forces us to make use of the terminology of magic), when Bredius, an excellent connoisseur of Dutch art, published in 1909 a pioneering monograph about the artist. Four years later the "Still Life with a Bridle" was discovered in quite unusual circumstances, which should not surprise us because it was like a last mockery from the other world. It served for several centuries as a cover for a barrel with raisins.

An anonymous reviewer writing in a 1922 publication about Viennese galleries reported a new work by Torrentius put up for sale; he described it as a real sensation, "Als ganz ausserordentliche Seltenheit." Its mythological subject was a peculiarity in itself; like nudes, it belonged to a rare genre in Dutch painting. In addition, what extreme audacity in his treatment of the subject. In the foreground a large, ornate bed, a baldachin with a fat cupid hanging above it; on the bed Mars and Venus are entirely preoccupied with each other. On the left side Vulcan appears with a net in his hand, intending to catch the divine couple in the act. Above, a group of Olympians watch the scene with delight, like spectators in a theater. A few more details: a little monkey squatting on the bed, a white Doberman pinscher. Under the bed, sandals and a night pot.

We know nothing of the further fate of this canvas nor its aesthetic qualities, aside from a general remark of the reviewer: "Es ist eine Feinmalerei." But even this inventory of personages and objects emanates an atmosphere of the boudoir and dissoluteness, powder, perfumes, and sin. Wasn't Torrentius far ahead of the style of his epoch, a solitary precursor of the rococo, a distant forerunner of Boucher and Fragonard? But in a country of sober-minded merchants, where did he find amateurs for his licentious works? Well, in almost every epoch there are collectors of obscene canvases who meticulously hide their treasures from the eyes of children, wives, and the guardians of morality. Only on exceptional occasions, excited by wine, will they wander with swaying steps toward their dark nooks and display them to their closest friends, bursting with an indecent giggle.

Only one painting was saved for us. One, and the only one stopped at the edge of nothingness.

2.

THE life of Torrentius is a ready literary fabric; it imposes a style, demands from the writer a rapid, breakneck narrative, sharp contrasts, baroque exaggeration, modeling of the protagonist from contradictory elements, and the art of expressing moods changing from lighthearted jauntiness and intoxication with the sensual world to the dread of the torture room and catastrophe. A bewitching subject.

It is much harder to manage his lonely work. It is homogeneous; at the same time it brings to mind a palimpsest and a subtly woven chain that leads to the bottom of a dark well of ever-new secrets. It lures us, and leads us astray.

An attempt to explain to anyone that the painting is a masterpiece seems quite hopeless, as usual in such cases. Art historians have not confirmed this with their word of honor, and I myself do not know how to translate my stifled shout when I first stood face-to-face with the "Still Life" into comprehensible language, nor the joyous surprise, the gratitude that I was endowed beyond measure, the soaring act of rapture.

I remember a certain episode that happened many years ago not far from Paris in an old monastery transformed into a retreat for intellectuals. A park, and in the park the ruins of a Gothic temple. The remains of the walls, white and thin as parchment, grew out of the ground. Their unreality was emphasized by the large, ogival windows through which light-hearted birds were flying. There were no longer stained-glass windows or columns, vaults or stone floors; only the skin of the architecture remained, as if hanging in the air. Inside the nave, fat pagan grass.

I remember this image better than the face of my interlocutor, Witold Gombrowicz, who was mocking my fondness for art. I did not even defend myself but only mumbled some nonsense, aware that I was only an object, a gymnast's bar upon which the writer was exercising his dialectical muscles. If I were an innocent stamp collector Gombrowicz would have made fun of my albums, classifiers, and sets of stamps; he would have proved that stamps are the lowest rungs of the ladder of existence, morally suspect.

"But it has absolutely no sense. How can one describe a cathedral, a sculpture, or some sort of painting," he asked me, quietly and pitilessly. "Leave this amusement to the historians of art. They don't understand anything either, but they have persuaded people they are cultivating a science." It sounded convincing. I know well, too well, all the agonies and vain effort of what is called description, and also the audacity of translating the wonderful language of painting into the language—as voluminous, as receptive as hell—in which court verdicts and love novels are written. I don't even know very well what inclines me to undertake these efforts. I would like to believe that it is my impervious ideal that requires me to pay it clumsy homages.

It seems Gombrowicz was irritated by the innate "stupidity" of the fine arts. Indeed, there is no painting that even in a popular way could demonstrate the philosophy of Kant, or Husserl and Sartre, two favorite thinkers of the writer who served him to intellectually annihilate interlocutors that were first subject, however, to the meticulous manipulation of what he called *upupienie*.

But this very "stupidity," or to speak more delicately, naïveté, has always put me in a state of happiness. Thanks to the intermediary of paintings, I experienced the grace of meeting the Ionian philosophers of nature. Concepts sprouted only from things. We spoke the simple language of the elements. Water was water, a rock was a rock, fire was fire. How good that the deadly abstractions had not drunk all the blood of reality to the end.

Paul Valéry warned: "We should apologize that we dare to speak about painting." I was always aware of committing a tactless act.

The "Still Life" of Torrentius was discovered quite accidentally in 1913, almost exactly three centuries after its creation. The painting has the monogram of the painter on its back, as well as a stamp stating it belonged to the collection of Charles I.

Helpless wonder is the most appropriate attitude toward the posthumous fate of this artist. We cannot help it. I could tell about many events that have happened to me since I decided to investigate this painter: the sudden piling up of insurmountable difficulties, the mysterious disappearance of my notes (precisely about him), misleading signals, books leading on a false track. Torrentius fiercely defended himself from the alms of charitable memory.

The "Still Life with a Bridle" is in the shape of a circle somewhat flattened "on the opposite poles," and creates the impression of a slightly concave mirror. Because of this mirror the objects assume an intensified and swollen reality. Torn from the environment that disturbs their peace, they lead a willful and majestic life. Our everyday, practical eye blurs contours and perceives only muddy, tangled traces of light. Painting invites us to the contemplation of individual, despised objects, it removes their banal accidentality; here an ordinary tumbler means more than it means—as if it were the sum of all tumblers, the essence of the species.

The light of the painting is peculiar: cold, cruel, one would like to say clinical. Its source is beyond the painted scene. A narrow shaft of brightness defines the figures with geometric precision, but it does not penetrate the depths, it stops before the smooth, hard wall of the background, black as basalt.

On the left side—but a literary description resembles the laborious moving of heavy furniture, it develops slowly in time while the painterly vision is sudden, given like a landscape seen in the illumination of lightning. On the left side, then, a clay jug with a warm, brown glaze on which a small circle of light has settled. In the middle the tumbler, called a *romer,* made of thick glass and half-filled with wine. Finally, a pewter pitcher with an energetically protruding beak. These three vessels, lined up facing the spectator in a position of attention, stand on a barely outlined shelf near two pipes with their stems turned down, and the lightest detail of the painting, a white-hot piece of paper with a musical score and text. At the top is the object I could not decipher at first, which seemed to be a piece of old armor hanging on the wall; at closer obser-

vation, it appeared to be a chain bridle used to tame exceptionally skittish horses. This metal contraption, stripped of its
stable commonness, emerges from the dark background
threatening, hieratic, somber like the specter of the Great
Commander.

Wonderfully misleading Torrentius jeers at all those investi-
gators who want to define his status and place in the history
of art. He could not fit within life; one looks vainly for him
in textbooks in which everything results from something and
everything falls in well-behaved patterns. One is certain that
in his generation he was an absolutely exceptional phenomenon without any definite artistic forebears, competitors, imita-
tors, or pupils, a painter bursting schematic divisions into
schools and trends.

This is probably why the not very clear title "master of illusory realism" was bestowed on him. What does it mean? Simply the rendering of people, objects, and landscapes so they
seem alive, not only deceptively similar but identical with the
model. The hand instinctively reaches out, wishing to liberate
from their frame existences that were put to sleep. The old
masters appealed not only to the eye, but also awakened other
senses: taste, smell, touch, even hearing. Thus in the presence
of their works we quite physically feel the sour taste of iron,
the cold smoothness of a glass, the tickling of a peach or cor-
duroy, the gentle warmth of clay pitchers, the dry eyes of the
prophets, bouquet from old books, the breeze of an approaching storm.

The composition of Torrentius's work is simple, almost ascetic. Built on horizontal and vertical axes, the painting is
based on the design of a cross; it would make a graceful subject for practitioners of formal analysis and their somewhat
pedantic search for parallels, diagonals, squares, circles, and
triangles. But in this case such exertions do not seem very
fruitful. From the beginning I had the irresistible impression

that in the motionless world of the picture something much more, and something very essential, is occurring. As if the represented objects combined in meaningful relations and the entire composition contained a message, an incantation transmitted in the letters of a forgotten language.

The "Still Life with a Bridle" is for many historians one of a number of extremely popular allegories, namely the allegory Vanitas. One can agree with this, because who would dare to oppose Ecclesiastes, who proclaims that everything is vanity of vanities. But this simple explanation sems too superficial, too general. How to explain, for instance, the exceedingly daring and "surrealist" juxtaposition in the picture of the bridle hanging menacingly over the trinity of vessels? Above all, that page with musical notes and a text. Maybe precisely here we should look for the hidden meaning of the work?

The text in Dutch is as follows:

> E R Wat buten maat bestaat
> int onmaats qaat verghaat.

The abbreviation used at the beginning of the verse can be read as "Eques Rosa Crucis," which brings us to the old scent—that is, the conjecture that Torrentius was a Rosicrucian. In fact, it is not a proof of anything. Equally well the artist could have painted this picture on commission from one of the members of the order, and according to his instructions. Similarly, during the Middle Ages an overwhelming majority of altar compositions were created according to strict indications from theologians who dictated to their artists the arrangement of scenes, symbols, even colors. Preserved contracts expressly attest to this.

Gnomic poems, particularly those that are esoteric texts, should be explained rather than translated word by word. One should approach them by degrees of meaning, carefully and on tiptoes, because literalness renders their meaning shallow and frightens away mystery.

Here is how I understand the text inscribed in Torrentius's painting:

> What exists beyond measure (order)
> in over-measure (disorder) will meet a bad end.

I realize this is one of several possible translations, and it sounds rather banal compared with the original, which shows a greater wealth of thought. However, the apparent obviousness of this translation should not be discouraging. Whoever has come in contact with the thought of the Pythagoreans or Neo-Platonism knows the large role played by the symbolism of numbers in these movements, also the measure of and the search for a mathematical formula uniting man with the cosmos.

The intellectual construction of the poem is based on the antinomy of harmony and chaos, or of reasonable form and shapeless matter, which in the cosmologies of many religions was a dark mass awaiting the divine act of creation. In ethical categories Torrentius's "Still Life" is not at all an allegory of Vanitas if my suppositions are correct, but an allegory of one of the cardinal virtues called Moderation, Temperantia, Sophrosyne. This interpretation is suggested by the represented objects: a bridle, the reins of the passions, vessels that give shape to formless liquids, and also the tumbler only half-filled as if recalling the praiseworthy custom of the Greeks of mixing wine with water.

Thus I had reasons to believe my exegesis of Torrentius's painting was very probable. Wasn't it clear, and logically cohesive? It had only one defect: precisely that suspicious simplicity.

So the poem inscribed in the painting did not leave me in peace, a poem that possessed a stonelike compactness and the finality of a sacred formula. To reach its philosophical sources I started to leaf through treatises by esoteric writers contemporary with the painter, above all Johann Valentin Andreae. *Fama Fraternitatis* and *Confessio* are the basis for learning the doctrine of the Fraternity. Then the work of the English physician Robert Fludd, who contributed much to popularizing the ideas of the Rosicrucians; the strange, intricate books of the alchemist Studion, who searched for the ideal dimensions of the Mystical Temple; and of course works by Jacob Boehme and Theophrast Bombastus of Hohenheim.

At the beginning the reading of hermetic books has a taste of Great Adventure; it is a marvelous wandering of uninitiated thought through exotic lands. The gray abstractions of philosophers are replaced by graceful symbols and images; everything connects with everything else and moves toward the desired Unity. The world becomes weightless and transparent. Provided you accept the first frail premise, provided you only adapt to the secret language, do not ask for definitions, put trust in the Method. To submit means to believe. How strange that the most obscure ideological obsessions take a similar course.

I think I had a sufficient supply of patience, even good will, but I lacked humility. It was my skeptical devil that guarded me from rapture and the grace of Illumination. I say this without pride, with a bit of regret. In the end there remained only a cool delectation. Without attaining initiation, spurned by the Mystery of the chosen, I fell into the hell of the aesthetes. Truly beautiful are those constructions of liberated minds: vertiginous pyramids of spirit, monuments of air, mirrorlike labyrinths of allegory, precious animals and stones; green jasper, the sign of luminosity; blue sapphire, truth; golden topaz, harmony.

These peregrinations over so many treatises were not at all wasted. I received important information from them. It is known that sects and secret societies base their doctrines on the teachings of a prophet-founder who radiates the attraction of an old tradition. For the Rosicrucians it was Christian Rosenkreutz, a German nobleman and knight-errant of gnosis who during a trip to the Holy Land, Damascus, Africa, and Spain acquired knowledge from Arab sages about the last things. As befits a prophet he lived long, 107 years (1378–1485). After returning to his country he founded a small order and devoted himself to occult studies. According to legend, 120 years after the master's death his body was discovered, untouched by decay, in an underground tomb in the shape of a chapel-sanctuary. The description of this sepulchral construction of which no trace has remained is like a guide through an imaginary museum of symbols: sculptures, inscriptions, a lamp that would be extinguished when a noninitiated person approached, old books, complicated geometrical figures on the floor, and ingenious vaults. With these objects of cult it seems mirrors were discovered in which the symbols of virtues were affixed in a miraculous manner. Hence the content of Torrentius's painting.

For several score years the Order of Rosicrucians led the secret life of the catacombs. During this period it feverishly looked for influential protectors, princes, and scholars; it founded international "lodges," gathered at secret conventicles, published anonymous tracts. Their caution was well-motivated, for the Fraternity was accused of close contacts with the Reformation, of decided hostility toward Rome, sympathies with the Arab and Jewish worlds, plans to overturn the established order, and of course contacts with unclean powers.

After a long period of incubation the Rosicrucians decided to begin open activity on a large scale. It was believed the appropriate moment had come to accomplish the work of transforming the world. It happened in the year 1614. At this time a famous pamphlet appeared, *Allgemeine und General Reformation der ganzen weiten Welt.* Is it just an accident that the "Still Life with a Bridle" bears precisely this date?

THIS is how I finished the first version of my essay about Torrentius. I put the manuscript away in a drawer. I secretly counted that time would work to my advantage. Investigation of difficult subjects requires alchemical patience.

A few years later, quite unexpectedly and without any action on my part, I received a parcel in the mail with a copy of a short, very learned treatise about my painter. A true gift from heaven and human good will. A letter sent from Holland had wandered senselessly through many countries and reached my hands in a pitiful state. Pages were stuck to each other or worn, sheets had greasy spots, the printing was smudged. I don't know who maltreated this innocent work, probably official Peeping Toms of other people's letters, and not gentlemen, which releases me from wasting time on an incident of menials. Luckily the text was bilingual; after difficult compilations I managed to understand its content. I could not get rid of the feeling that whoever falls into Torrentius's snares must be ready for anything.

The author of this treatise, the Dutch historian of art and music Pieter Fischer, draws attention for the first time to the musical page in the "Still Life," those notes and a small score inscribed in the painting. Until now this was generally thought to be a decorative element—a simple ornament—and that there was no connection between the notes and the text below. Fischer proves that such a connection exists, and that it has to be discovered to better understand the meaning of the work.

It is indeed surprising that no one noticed the evident mistake in Torrentius's couplet. Everyone, absolutely everyone, read the word *quaat* (evil), while in the painting it is clearly, black on white, *qaat*. One could say the painter was not very strong in orthography, were it not for the fact that above this word is a note that breaks harmony (h and not b, as it should be). It is therefore an intended, completely conscious, double mistake of orthography and music, an infraction of the principles of language and melody. A symbolic violation of order. In the Middle Ages this musical-moralistic procedure bore the name *diabolus in musica,* and it usually accompanied the word *peccatum.*

Fischer's interpretation of the text itself, the couplet, seems less convincing. The author believes that the abbreviation "E R" opening the poem signifies Extra Ratione, which prompts him to reel off further bold hypotheses. A painter with such a scandalous life who challenged the world could not be an apologist of restraint. The "Still Life with a Bridle" should be understood as an apparent allegory of moderation, while in reality, in an intricately camouflaged way, it is the praise of a man liberated from bonds, uncommon, standing high above the crowd of petty philistines.

In the English catalogue of the Rijksmuseum I found a different version of the disquieting poem from Torrentius's painting. It is not a literal translation, but one of the possible attempts to understand the hermetic text: "That which is extraordinary has an extraordinary bad fate." It sounds too explicit, rather flat, and it is not certain why a prophetic gift is ascribed to the artist, a foreboding of his ill-fated end.

Finally, one should pose the question whether Torrentius's work—so splendidly substantial and classically self-enclosed—really demands complex explanations that overstep the framework of its autonomous world. It is indifferent to us which spirits, good or evil, wise or reckless, inspired the painter's work. After all, the painting does not live by the reflected glow of secret books and treatises. It has its own light, the clear, penetrating light of clarity.

IT is time to part with Torrentius. I studied him long enough to admit my ignorance with a clear conscience. I suspect I put a defensive mechanism into motion, as if fearing that from this truly tragic history a figure of an ordinary adventurer would emerge. I did not want it, so I collected proofs he was an unusual man bursting measures and standards, systematically and with stubbornness worthy of a martyr's palm.

As a legacy he left us an allegory of restraint, a work of

105

great discipline, self-knowledge, and order, contradicting his reckless existential experience. But only simpletons and naive moralizers demand exemplary harmony of life and work from an artist.

We will probably never learn who he really was. A victim of a political conspiracy? The flagrant disproportion of crime and punishment, the resonance of the trial and diplomatic intervention, all indicate this. Could the vindictiveness of the husbands and fathers of seduced women go as far as judicial murder? What was his connection with the Rosicrucians? One cannot altogether rule out that his scandalous excesses were a misleading maneuver, a mask concealing the conspiratorial activity of a member of the Fraternity. Perhaps he was a peculiar ascetic à rebours—they appear not only in Russian novels—who by his fall and sin aims in a roundabout way at the highest good.

So many questions. I did not manage to break the code. The enigmatic painter, the incomprehensible man, begins to pass from the plane of investigation based on flimsy sources to an indistinct sphere of fantasy, the domain of tellers of tales. Thus it is time to part with Torrentius.

Farewell, still life.

Good night, severed head.

THE NONHEROIC
SUBJECT

❏

DUTCH painting speaks many languages, it tells about the matters of earth and of heaven. It lacks only one thing: the immortalization of the moments of its defeat and glory, the apotheosis of its own history. After all, it was a history abundant in dramatic episodes, insurrections, terror, sieges, struggles with powerful adversaries such as England, Spain, and France.

When Dutch artists painted war it was the war of light and darkness, also the smooth water of the canals with a solitary mill on the shore, an ice rink under the pink sky of sunset, the interior of a pub with shouting drunkards, a girl reading a letter. If other testimony had not been preserved we could think that the inhabitants of this low-lying country led a truly sweet life—they ate richly, drank copiously, and enjoyed cheerful company. In vain do we look for works by prominent painters that transmit to posterity the execution of Hoorn and of Egmont, the heroic defense of Leyden, or the assassination attempt against Wilhelm of Orange named "The Silent."

In his beautiful book *The Old Masters* Eugène Fromentin draws our attention to an unusual fact. In times pregnant with historical events, "a young man painted a bull on a pasture, another one who wished to please his friend—a physician—painted him in a dissecting room surrounded by his pupils and with a scalpel stuck in the arm of a corpse. These two paintings covered their names, their centuries and the country where they lived with immortal fame. What is it then that wins our gratitude? Is it dignity and truth? No. Is it greatness? Sometimes. And maybe beauty itself? Always beauty."

This is very nicely said, but it is doubtful that the pacifistic spirit of Dutch painting can be explained in purely aesthetic terms. What, then, is behind this peculiar predilection for scenes from everyday life? Why did the Dutch avoid war subjects that exalt patriotic feelings? It seems the problem is much more profound; we must summon the aid of history, which molded the psychology of this nation.

Let us recall one of the most famous episodes in the Dutch struggles for freedom, the defense of Leyden, as it was described by a chronicler of the times, Emanuel van Materen.

Six years of the rule of the Prince of Alba, of terror and violence, did not succeed in breaking the resistance of the Netherlanders. The northern part of the country defended itself with particular fierceness. With the help of mercenaries, the Prince of Orange organized armed expeditions against the Spaniards, and the fighting continued with changing fortunes. After the long, drawn-out, heroic defense of Haarlem, when all means and supplies were exhausted, he capitulated to Alba's army. But the invaders did not manage to seize Alkmar; they were compelled to end the siege of the city ingloriously.

The war in the Netherlands did not follow the usual course of events, or the traditional ritual of pitched battles on a large plain ending with only victors and those who beg for pity. Rather it was a general rebellion, a levy en masse of the entire nation—peasants, bourgeois, and nobility—against Spanish violence. It burst out like fire in different spots, died down but not completely, and flared up anew. The powerful army of occupation was constantly taken by surprise, and unable to deal a decisive blow.

In the beginning of the war a Spanish officer, unaware he was challenging fate, called the Dutch insurgents beggars *(gueux)*. These mendicants proved to be dangerous and invincible adversaries. Insurgents from the forest and ocean, especially the latter, whose bravery would be celebrated for centuries in folk song, attacked enemy convoys and even conquered ports, slaughtering the Spanish crews. "The red sun blazes over Holland," said one of the poets of the times.

Toward the end of 1573, Philip II recalled the Prince of Alba to Spain from his position as Commander in Chief in the Netherlands, the equivalent of disgrace. Always and everywhere the politics of terror proves to be the politics of the blind. His successor, Don Luis de Requesens, tried to win the rebels over with acts of grace, tax reductions, and amnesty, but he never gave up his intention of forcing the unyielding North to its knees.

In May 1574, the Spanish Army came to Leyden. The fathers of the city unanimously decided to defend themselves, issuing a series of indispensable military and administrative decrees. The question of a just distribution of food was regulated at the beginning; during the first two months of the siege, every inhabitant of Leyden received half a pound of bread and milk (separated milk, as the scrupulous chronicler reports). At the time Leyden was not a large city. It had certain rustic features—for example, large stables and barns with more than 700 cows. The problem of feed for the animals was solved very cleverly; taking advantage of the Spaniards' inattention the cattle were led to nearby meadows, but as soon as sounds of war and shots were heard the animals galloped back to the city. During the entire siege only one cow and three absentminded calves were put on the list of losses.

The commander of the Spaniards, General Valdez, waited

for the city to fall into his hands, captured either by hunger or a stratagem. It seems he trusted diplomacy more than artillery, at least in the initial phase of the clash. He sent letters to the defenders assuring them they could count on his magnanimity and forgiveness, and that the Spanish Army would not remain in the city for long. At the end he perversely argued that the submission of the fortress would not bring shame or loss of honor to anyone, while conquest by force would disgrace the unfortunate defenders.

Vain efforts. The inhabitants of Leyden were resolved to persist in their noble resistance. Valdez received a Latin poem in reply; its translation reads as follows:

> The flute of the fowler luringly sings
> Until the bird falls into the net's strings.

In September, after four months of fighting, the situation of the city became more critical each day. Witty poems no longer occurred to anyone. This time the defenders answered the repeated proposal of capitulation with a pathetic letter: "You place all your hope on the fact that we are hungry, and no relief comes to us. You call us eaters of cats and dogs, but as long as the mooing of cows is heard in the city we do not lack food. And when we will lack food, each of us has his left hand; we can cut it off, preserving the right hand to push the tyrant and his bloody horde away from the city walls."

At Leyden as at Troy there were speeches by leaders, brilliant replies, and deadly insults. All this flowery rhetoric seemed to be destined for the authors of future history textbooks. The truth was prosaic, banal, and gray—to persevere and survive one more month, one more week, one more day.

An acute lack of currency was felt in the city, so they decided to adapt the monetary system to the exceptional situation. Special paper banknotes were issued that would preserve value only during the period of siege. These new means of payment were decorated with slogans intended to comfort the defenders' hearts: a Latin inscription, *Haec libertas ego,* a picture of a lion, and a pious sigh, "May the Lord protect Leyden."

It was evident to everyone, however, that the city could be saved only with help from the outside. Hunger was increasing, there was no more bread. Meat, or rather the skin and bones of emaciated animals, was still rationed at half a pound per person; people hunted dogs, cats, and rats.

To make things worse, a plague broke out. Within a short period it swallowed up six thousand victims, which was half the population of the city. The men were so weakened that they had no strength to keep guard on top of the walls; when they returned home, they often found their wives and children dead.

As if these misfortunes were not enough, rioting broke out in Leyden. The chronicler speaks enigmatically about disagreement, muttering, and disputes. We can easily guess what was concealed beneath these euphemisms. It was simply a rebellion of the city's poor, the ones who felt the burden of the siege the most painfully. They had only two alternatives— death from hunger, or slavery—and they were choosing the latter.

The mayor called all the population of the city to a public meeting. In a great, pathetic speech he announced that he was ready to offer his body to feed the hungry. Luckily, his statement was taken as it should be, not as a concrete offer but as a rhetorical figure.

The Estates General and Wilhelm Prince of Orange, Commander in Chief of the Dutch Army quartered in nearby Delft, were aware that the situation in Leyden was fatal. The land army of the Prince of Orange was too weak to relieve the city and wage a battle with the enemy on firm ground.

The strongest and most competent part of the armed forces of the Netherlands was the navy, but there was a serious obstacle: Leyden was not a port, it was situated inland. For aid—this rings almost magically—it was necessary to call on the element of water.

A careful plan to break the dikes and dams was worked out. The Dutch system of canals resembled a labyrinth of water, and woe to those who dared cross its frontiers. The decision to drown large tracts of arable fields and pastures was dramatic; consolation was found in folk wisdom, and in an old peasant proverb that said that in such extreme situations it is better to make soil barren than lose it forever.

In the shipyards of Rotterdam and other ports, feverish labor was in full swing. The giddy speed of building ships to take part in the operation of liberating Leyden is worthy of admiration, even for us who live in a technological era. The entire flotilla was composed of two hundred galleys with a shallow draught; moved by the force of the wind or oars, they were equipped with cannons and all the necessary equipment for war.

Everything now depended on one unpredictable factor—the weather. At first an unfavorable Nord was blowing; soon, however, the longed-for southwestern wind began to blow, and, through openings in the dikes, pushed masses of water toward Leyden. The offensive of the element preceded the offensive of the armed forces.

The adversary was completely taken aback. The Spaniards tried to control the situation, hurriedly repairing the broken dikes, but the Dutch galleys stormed through, firing with all their cannons. In places where the water was not sufficiently deep, the crews jumped from the ships and pushed them in the direction of the enemy's entrenchments. Here was a great subject for a baroque painting: If Rubens had painted this battle he would probably have represented it as a struggle of Neptune with the chthonic deities.

The Spanish Army was unable to take advantage of its numerical superiority or tactical abilities. A land army that stands up to its knees in water fighting against a navy is a pure absurdity. There was only one way out—a quick raising of the siege and inglorious retreat. On the third of September 1574, at eight in the morning, Admiral Louis Boisot, commander of the Dutch soldiers who came with relief, entered the gates of the city to an enthusiastic welcome.

What remains in today's Leyden of these days of suffering and glory? A statue of the brave mayor, Pieter Andriaas van der Werf, in the shade of old plane trees. His coat is thrown over his shoulders as if he were on his way to an ordinary city council meeting; only the rapier at his side indicates that the matters decided at the time were of life and death.

In the park there is also an old tower with a huge piece of wall chipped off by Spanish cannons during the last night of siege. A nice house decorated with images of birds recalls those times, and has been preserved. Three brothers lived there, Jan, Ulrich, and Willem, city musicians by profession whose hobby was breeding carrier pigeons. During the siege they happened to play a particularly important role. They almost became an institution, in a dual way—a postal ministry because they maintained the only possible contact with the external world during the siege, and an office of propaganda because the pigeons were tireless ambassadors of hope, promising quick relief to the defenders.

In the Leyden Museum there is a large tapestry representing the attack of the Dutch flotilla against the Spanish entrenchments. Seen with the eye of a cartographer it is a huge green plain cut by the blue lines of rivers and canals, people small as insects busily moving between them. History from the perspective of God.

In the same museum we find neither cannons nor enemy standards, neither chipped swords nor cleft helmets. In a word, none of the esteemed bric-a-brac that one finds in other European collections devoted to great events of the past. On the other hand, a peculiar war trophy hangs in the place of honor: a large copper cauldron, used to cook food for soldiers, left by the Spaniards in their flight. A cauldron as a symbol of the return to normalcy, or if someone prefers, a symbol of victory.

DURING the eighty years of fighting for independence the Dutch gave countless proofs of courage, perseverance, and determination. But this long war was not like any other that took place in Europe. It was a clash of two different ideals of life, two systems of values, and, one might say with a certain exaggeration, two diametrically different civilizations: the military aristocracy of the Spaniards, and the bourgeois-peasant world of the Netherlanders.

It is worthwhile to mention a characteristic detail. The chronicler of the Leyden defense says with evident satisfaction that during the assault, when the dikes in the direct neighborhood of the city were destroyed, only five or six men were killed. Such a negligible number of victims would not have attracted the attention of other European historians.

For the Dutch, war was not a beautiful craft, an adventure of youth, or the crowning of a man's life. They undertook it without exaltation but also without protest, as one enters a struggle with an element. According to such a code of behavior, there was no room for displays of heroic bravery or spectacular death on the field of glory. On the contrary, what was most important was to save: to protect, to spare, and carry from the storm a sane head and one's belongings.

The brutal force of the Spanish army of occupation was thus counteracted with intelligence, a strict merchant's calculation, organizational talents, and finally a stratagem. True, these were not knightly virtues. If the Dutch modeled themselves on the heroes of the great epics, surely Odysseus was closer to them than Achilles.

But there is no need to reach for mythology. The character and structure of Dutch society explain a lot; the men of war in Holland did not form a separate social class surrounded by a nimbus of fame or enjoying special prestige. The nobility, which in the rest of Europe formed an officer corps with centuries-old traditions, did not play a great role in the Republic. A young man who enlisted in the army as a soldier did not carry in his backpack a staff of office (if one may use such an anachronism), but the bitter bread of the poor, with no prospects that fortune would ever smile on him. When sick or wounded, he usually died in a shabby field hospital where epidemics were raging. Veterans begged in the city streets.

Holland did not have a fixed number of soldiers. The army was not a school to mold the spirit of its citizens, as with the Romans; the prestige of the state consisted in something entirely different. Hence a purely functional attitude toward the armed forces: during war the land army numbered a little more than a hundred thousand soldiers; during peace it fell to twenty thousand.

In the army of the Republic most of the land forces were foreign mercenaries; only the navy was "purely" Dutch. The sons of Mars were simply bought. At the siege of s'Hertogenbosch, during the decisive phase of the battle for freedom, the army commanded by Vice Regent Frederick Henry was composed of three Dutch regiments (they were not at all volunteers), and fifteen regiments of Fresians, Walloons, Germans, French, Scotch, and English. In addition, this medley did not wear uniforms. A helmet, armor plate, sometimes a sash with the colors of the detachment—all of this was very gray in comparison with the feathered splendor of the French or Italian warriors. There was nothing to paint.

Memories of wars paled quickly. The one who ordered a

painting—ship captain, peasant, merchant, or artisan—wanted above all to see himself and the world that surrounded him: the house interior where the family gathered for the occasion of a baptism or wedding, a country road lined with trees and the glow of the afternoon sun falling on them, or a native town on a big plain.

Therefore it was not a very patriotic art, if by the word patriotism we understand the fierce hatred of all old, present, and even potential enemies. The Dutch did not leave us a single painting where a defeated adversary is dragged behind a victor's chariot in the dust of spite.

Yet they painted sea battles with such delight. The classical example of this genre is the work of Hendrik Vroom, "Battle at Gibraltar on April 25, 1607." In the foreground a Dutch warship pierces the hull of a Spanish flagship with its prow. The painting is small, and to speak in a not very tactful way, full of delightful details: red and yellow braids of explosions, people, remnants of masts flying into the air and drowning in the sea, thousands of small touches rendered with a miniature painter's precision. And all this seen as if through a telescope, from a distant perspective that dissolves horror and passion. A battle changed into a ballet, a colorful spectacle.

In one of his letters to Madame de Staël, Benjamin Constant enthusiastically speaks of Holland's history, so different from that of other European countries: "This brave nation never declared war on its neighbors, never invaded, never devastated or plundered their lands." (Constant passes in discreet silence over the colonial conquests, he speaks only about neighbors.) This remark of a French writer puts an essential feature of the Dutch character into relief. Someone said: "La Hollande est de religion d'Erasme." It would not be a great exaggeration to say that the spirit of the philosopher from Rotterdam, who valued the virtues of moderation and gentleness above everything else, took power over this small nation.

*   *   *

ONE winter morning during a stroll in Berlin's Grunewald, I dropped by the Hunter's Castle. I knew for a long time that it housed a collection of Flemish and Dutch paintings. I entered partly out of duty, not expecting any revelations. I felt I would see one more mediocre collection (O the monotony of the second-rate painters of Great Schools!): portraits, hunting scenes, still lifes that hang on the walls of so many aristocratic residences. This is indeed what happened.

But I did not regret the visit, because I discovered what I had sought in so many representative galleries and museums for a long time. The painting was not a masterpiece at all, but its subject drew my attention: "Allegory of the Dutch Republic." It was painted by Jacob Andriaensz Backer, and for his work he received the not trifling sum of 300 guldens from the hands of Frederick Henry, Vice Regent of the United Provinces. Therefore, it was something like an official work.

The painting represents a young girl dressed in draperies of intense colors: red, blue, and a luminous pearly white. The model has a country look: the pink cheeks of a shepherdess, round shoulders, monumental legs firmly resting on the ground. Upon this personification of simplicity, freedom, and innocence the artist has imposed the heavy attributes of war: a helmet with a thick black plume, a shield in one hand and an operatic spear in the other. This is precisely what is most attractive in the painting: the contradiction between the elevated subject and its modest expression, as if a historical drama was played by a country troupe at a fair. The heroine of the scene does not resemble at all "Freedom leading people onto the barricades." Soon she will leave the boring task of posing and go to her everyday, nonpathetic occupations in a stable or on a haystack.

Freedom—so many treatises were written about it that it became a pale, abstract concept. But for the Dutch it was something as simple as breathing, looking, and touching objects. It did not need to be defined or beautified. This is why there is no division in their art between what is great and what is small, what is important and unimportant, elevated and ordinary. They painted apples and the portraits of fabric shopkeepers, pewter plates and tulips, with such patience and such love that the images of other worlds and noisy tales about earthly triumphs fade in comparison.

APOCRYPHAS

❑

THE MERCY OF THE
EXECUTIONER

❑

AMONG the many portraits of Jan van Oldenbarneveldt I like most the one painted by an unknown master. The Great Pensionary is shown as an old man. Even the paint's substance carries the marks of disintegration, of mold, dust, and cobweb. Though not a beautiful face, it is full of expression and noble strength: a very high forehead, a large, meaty, not very shapely nose, a patriarchal beard, and under bushy eyebrows intelligent eyes where the desperate energy of someone trapped is glowing.

No historian denies that Oldenbarneveldt was one of the most meritorious founders of the new Republic. He was called Holland's defender. This first great politician, who came from the middle classes and represented their interests, knew how to defend the rights of the young state better than anyone else. He negotiated with the powerful monarchs of Spain, France, and England, prepared advantageous armistices, peace treaties, and alliances, and during the forty years of his life worked faithfully and untiringly for his country. But with the approach of old age his political sense began to fail. Oldenbarneveldt made crucial mistakes, and the culmination of these was a "sharp resolution" allowing towns to recruit mercenaries not subject to orders from the Prince of Orange, the true commander of the Republic's army. The country was on the threshold of civil war.

Oldenbarneveldt not only lost all sense of judgment in the situation, but his instinct of self-preservation abandoned him as well. He did not understand, or did not want to understand, that his handful of supporters was melting away and everyone was against him—the governor, the Estates General, and the towns. Returning home from his office, he stepped with indifference over leaflets written against him. He did not listen to the advice of friends, who insisted that he resign and go abroad. He was like a large, old turtle dying on the sand, sinking deeper and deeper.

The finale was easy to guess, and surprising only to Oldenbarneveldt himself. Arrested after a months-long investigation, he stood before a special tribunal composed mostly of his enemies. Deprived of a lawyer, he furiously defended his honor rather than his life.

The time of the action: May 13, 1619. Place: The Hague, Binnenhof—a brick Gothic and Renaissance decoration of the drama. In the courtyard a wooden scaffold was hastily erected and sand strewn about. It was late afternoon. The fiery carriage of Helios—as rhetorical poets write—rolled westward. When they brought in the condemned man, the crowd fell silent. Oldenbarneveldt was hurrying toward death: "What you must do, do it fast," he urged the executors of the verdict.

Then something happened that went far beyond the ritual of execution, beyond the procedure of any known execution. The executioner led the condemned man to a spot where sunlight was falling and said, "Here, Your Honor, you will have sun on your face."

One might ask the question whether the executioner who cut off the head of the Great Pensionary was a good executioner. The goodness of the executioner depends on his ability to carry out his task quickly, efficiently, and in an impersonal way. Who more than he deserves to be called the executor of fate, or the soundless lightning of destiny? His virtues should be silence and cool restraint. He should administer the blow without hatred, without compassion, without any kind of emotion.

Oldenbarneveldt's executioner broke the rules of the game, left his role, and, what is more, violated the principles of professional ethics. Why did he do it? Certainly it was an impulse of the heart. But didn't the condemned man, who was stripped of all earthly glory, perceive derision in it? After all, it is indifferent to those who are leaving forever whether they die in the sun, in shadow, or the darkness of night. The executioner, artisan of death, became an ambiguous figure filled with potential meaning when to the condemned man—in his last moment—he threw a crumb of helpless goodness.

THE CAPTAIN

❑

ON December 28th, 1618, the sailboat *New Horn* left port on Texel Island, setting out on the long, dangerous journey to East India. The cargo was barrels of gunpowder. The ship's captain, Willem Ysbrants Bontekoe, has described the history of this peculiar navigation.

His simple, severe, and at the same time naive narrative should be considered reliable. The only doubt comes from the way he presented an important episode of the expedition, especially because three different versions of the event have reached us that contradict one another.

Gales, lulls at sea, storms lasting several days, tropical downpours recalling the biblical deluge and sicknesses afflicting the crew, skirmishes with Spaniards—all this was daily bread for the sailors and contained within the limits of what was considered normal. This norm was overstepped on the nineteenth of November 1619, in open sea and far from the goal of the journey.

That day Captain Bontekoe must have been in good humor; he ordered a double portion of aqua vitae to be given to the crew with its evening meal. Plunging into the darkness of the hold with a tallow candle's brightness, the mate in charge of food supplies pours alcohol from a barrel into a bucket. The weather is stormy. A sudden list of the ship, the candle falls straight into the open barrel of spirit. A moment of liberation of elemental force—then everything happens according to the logic of catastrophes. An avalanche of events rapidly succeeds each other until the culminating point, the powerful explosion annihilating the ship.

A small part of the crew is saved in a lifeboat and wanders over the ocean under a sail made of shirts. They have neither water nor food, drink their own urine, eat the raw meat of flying fish. The pitiless sun of the tropics consumes the mind, giving birth to a barbarian desire to kill a ship's boy and feed on his flesh and blood.

Captain Bontekoe sits at the back of the boat. With his arms he shades his head from the heat. He has a high fever and is delirious. But what happens now in front of his eyes is not delirium but reality. With his left hand the sailor called Red Joost grabs the hair of a ship's boy, who screams as if he were insane—armed with a knife, Joost's right hand rises in the air. Let us freeze this image.

According to the first version, Captain Bontekoe rose and delivered a long speech full of biblical citations. He spoke of Isaac's sacrifice, which as we know God rejected, about the Ten Commandments, the duty to love one's brother, and so on and so on. A surrealistic picture presents itself: a black pulpit hovering over the endless expanse of salty waters. In fact the boat, left to the mercy of the waves, was not the stony nave of a cathedral, and the handful of mad, shipwrecked sailors in no way recalled well-fed, festively bedecked burghers gathered for a Sunday service. The moment did not lend itself at all to displays of pious rhetoric. In order to prevent murder, one had to act quickly, decidedly, and violently.

The second report says that Bontekoe managed to convince Joost and restrain him from executing his criminal plan. They made a pact: If they did not manage to reach solid land in three days, the boy would be killed. That three-day deadline (the magic number three) was not based on any rational premises, because no one even vaguely knew the position of the boat. Besides, if the captain settled the matter this way, it was equivalent to consent to murder, and in fact meant only deferral of the sentence. Bontekoe took the side of the murderers; in a way he accepted their arguments.

Finally, the third version, and the one most probable. The captain jumps to his feet and shouts that whoever dares touch the boy will not receive his daily pay and food ration; when they return to Amsterdam he will be hanged in front of the city walls on the highest gallows. This was a completely abstract threat if one takes into consideration the hopeless situation of the shipwrecked men, but its effect was staggering. To the sailors, mad with thirst and hunger, it restored a sense of moral order and presented before them a clear image of civilization: its foundation of food, money, and a wooden pole with a cross-beam at the top.

LONG GERRIT

❏

GERRIT was born in a small village near Veere, and like all the men in his family he was destined for the vocation of fisherman. In the normal course of events, after a laborious life he would pass his boat and house on to his sons, while he would be content with two yards of bitter soil. But nature, which is usually so careful in allotting shapes to all its creatures, made him different. To the distress of his parents, he grew beyond measure; at seventeen he reached the height of eight feet and five inches. Undoubtedly he was the tallest man that ever walked Dutch soil. In a mountainous country it might have been somewhat concealed; here, on a broad plain, his height was a constant though unintended provocation.

Endowed with huge strength, he was normally quiet, gentle, and sad. He did not have friends; girls shunned him. Most of all he liked to sit in the corner of a room and watch how the dust of the earth swirled in a beam of sunlight.

Not particularly held back by his parents, Gerrit decided to set forth in the world and make a profession of his anomaly. He wandered from village to village, from town to town; at country fairs or popular holidays he broke horseshoes, bent iron bars, threw barrels full of beer into the air lightly as balls, and stopped a galloping horse with his naked hands. He competed hard with other wonders of nature: a pig with two heads, a six-legged dog, a horse that knew how to count, as well as magicians, tightrope walkers, swallowers of melted sulfur, and clowns with stuffed bellies who fell facedown in the mud.

Amid charlatans, fortune-tellers, and rat catchers, in a deafening racket of drums, trumpets, and the shouts of dancing processions, in the smells of meat, garlic, and sweet pastry Gerrit towered high above like a mast—and let us admit it, he earned little. In his blue eyes lurked the worry of a father of a numerous family; Gerrit's numerous family was his huge, never-satiated body.

One autumn morning of 1688, Long Gerrit was found in an alley not far from Nieuwe Gracht in Haarlem. He was lying with his face down. His doublet was soaked in rain and blood, he had been stabbed repeatedly with a knife. Most likely there were many murderers, and the cotton pouch with money on his chest led one to believe it was not a robbery. The body was given to the University of Leyden, so he did not even have a decent burial. A few preachers, however, mentioned the murder in their sermons; one of them who was carried away by rhetorical fervor said Gerrit was dealt as many blows as Julius Caesar. It is not clear why this elevated analogy was used.

Perhaps the preacher wanted us to understand that the healthy republican spirit bestows equal hatred on giants and on caesars.

PORTRAIT IN A
BLACK FRAME

❏

I DON'T know why they kept choosing me, these elderly men
who sat next to me in bars, cafés, on benches in parks. They
made me listen to long monologues interspersed with the
names of exotic islands and oceans. Who were they? Bankrupts, stripped of wealth and power. They played the role of
exiled princes with the skill and routines of old actors. To
their credit it must be said they were not sentimental. They
knew they could not count on either applause or compassion;
they separated themselves from the surrounding world with
haughty spite.

They belonged to the same race and constituted what could
be called a specific kind of human species. They were betrayed
by predatory faces, also by clothes that had an old-fashioned,
frayed elegance: a hat with a fantastic shape rescued from a
deluge, a handkerchief in the breast pocket, a tie with a large
pearl, a silk scarf that had aged with them and now recalled
a rope wrapped around the neck.

As I listened to their tales I thought of a young twenty-year-
old man who in 1607, a few days after Christmas, left on a
ship of the Company of the Indies for the Far East. He was
Jan Pieterszoon Coen, the son of a small merchant from

Hoorn. Quite a task awaited him: inspecting the Dutch colonies in Java and the Moluccas, sending reports about prospects for commerce and the political situation in this faraway land where the influences of great colonial empires rubbed against one another. Such was the beginning of an epic, innocent and without significance.

It is difficult to say what prompted the Gentlemen of the Company to select this very young man without much experience. Was it the blind chance of fate, or was it his face that decided the choice, a face with the traits of a Spanish warrior that we know from later portraits: stubborn, domineering, an impenetrable face.

The colonies were doing badly. Coen informed the Company of this in numerous reports, written with passion and the zeal of an apostle of white civilization. The population was demoralized and uncertain of its fate; stores, banking houses, forts, and harbors were in a deplorable state, corruption and drunkenness had reached appalling dimensions. All this took place before the eyes of the natives, who were waiting for the appropriate moment to cut the throats of the invaders.

This is why Coen demanded weapons and an army. "Your Excellencies," he wrote in one of his letters to the Company, "should know that we cannot conduct war without commerce, nor commerce without war." He also requested young, morally irreproachable and hardworking Dutch to be sent to the colonies. They would replace the degenerate desperadoes. He asked his superiors—it was an unheard-of thing—to send fourteen-year-old girls from Dutch orphanages who in the future would become virtuous wives for the colonizers.

Bursting with energy and ideas, omnipresent, tirelessly sailing between Borneo, Sumatra, the Celebes, and Java, Coen united in his personality the traits of a member of the Tribunal of Holy Inquisition and a conquistador. He was thirty when he was nominated governor-general of East India, a position that put almost unlimited power in his hands. Historical experience teaches us that it leads as a rule to crime.

It happened that a young ensign, Cortenhoeff, was caught flirting with a twelve-year-old pupil of Governor Saartje Specx. They were both natural children of the Company's employees, a couple of teenagers without a home or love. Personally and cold-bloodedly, Coen dictated a death sentence against them.

The affair of the expedition against the islands of Ambon and Banda became well known in Europe. During a military campaign fourteen out of fifteen thousand inhabitants of these islands were murdered, and seven hundred sold into slavery. Some maintain that the real cause of the massacre was the local governor, Sonck, and Coen only gave the order for evacuation of the natives. The word "evacuation" was understood as a final evacuation and removal to the other world. Such semantic misunderstandings occur only in countries ruled by an iron hand.

The solitude of the strong man: Coen did not have friends. Strictly speaking he had only one; it was a shameful and deeply hidden friendship.

The great governor sneaked out at night with no bodyguard, walked the narrow streets of Batavia that were built like Amsterdam (steep roofs on the houses, canals, bridges, senseless mills milling the tropical heat), and would reach a rather dingy building where the Chinese Souw Bing Kong lived, a former ship captain and now banker—to speak more precisely, a moneylender.

What did they talk about? About accounting, which was the hidden passion, even the love of the governor. Bing Kong would reveal the secrets of the Chinese method of business bookkeeping, and Coen would sing the charms of Italian bookkeeping. After a day filled with hard work, the administrator of the Dutch colony felt relief, comfort, almost a physical happiness when he thought of the white sheets of paper and two columns of numbers under the rubrics "owes" and "has"; they ordered a complex, dark world just like the ethical categories of good and evil. Bookkeeping for Coen was the highest form of poetry—it liberated the hidden harmony of things.

He died in the prime of life, struck by tropical fever. The end came so suddenly he had no time to prepare a testament, or give last instructions. One might say he choked on death, but did not drink it to the end. This is probably why for long centuries he took the shape of other predators, all the way up to those I met in bars, in coffeehouses, and on park benches, the last of the species.

THE HELL OF
INSECTS

❑

JAN SWAMMERDAM was frail and sickly since birth. He was
kept alive only by the art of two eminent physicians. But efforts to awaken his sleepy humors brought no results. In
school he studied well but without enthusiasm; he did not
show any definite interests. His father owned the prospering
pharmacy By the Swan next to the town hall in Amsterdam;
soon he became reconciled to the thought—but not without
regret—that after his death his beautiful shop filled with
smells of botany and chemistry, a collection of natural oddi-
ties, and a crocodile hanging from the ceiling, would pass into
the hands of a stranger.

After long hesitation Jan decided to study medicine at the
University of Leyden. The family praised his intention and
promised appropriate material aid, nourishing the quiet hope
that a change of environment and scholarly discipline would
positively influence and toughen the wishy-washy character of
their only child.

Jan succumbed to the charms of knowledge, and in an exaggerated way—he studied everything. He attended lectures on
mathematics, theology, and astronomy; he did not neglect
seminars where they read texts of ancient authors; he was also

enthusiastic about Oriental languages. He gave the least attention to his chosen domain of knowledge, medicine.

"God is sorely trying your father," wrote Jan's mother, "adding worries about his son's fate to the torments of old age. You are wasting the priceless time of youth as if wandering through a forest instead of pursuing a straight path toward your goal. If within two years you do not receive a doctor's diploma, your father will stop sending money. Such is his will."

Jan finished medicine. But during his entire life he did not dress a single wound. The new passion that never left him until death was the study of the world of insects. Entomology did not yet exist as a separate domain of science; Jan Swammerdam established its foundations.

However, the study of the antennae of the dung beetle, of the digestive system of the wasp, of the legs of the mosquito did not bring Jan either revenue or fame. To make things worse, he was convinced he was wasting his life, devoting it to a barren and useless occupation. Religious, with inclinations toward mysticism, Swammerdam suffered because the objects of his studies were creatures on the lowest rung of the ladder of species, on the garbage heap of nature, in a neighborhood close to the hot vestibule of hell. Who can perceive God's finger in the anatomy of a louse? Is not the one-day damsel fly a splinter of nothingness rather than a permanent brick of existence? Therefore he envied astronomers, who could study the movements of planets and discover the architecture of the universe, the laws of harmony, and the will of the Eternal.

At night he was visited by messengers from the Heavens. They gently persuaded him to abandon his frivolous occupations. Swammerdam did not defend himself, only apologized. He promised to reform, but he knew he would never have the courage to burn his manuscripts, his beautiful, precise drawings and observations. Angels who know the secrets of the heart left him, and then a pandemonium would begin: small creatures flying low, crawling on the ground, with devils' faces and the devil's fierceness; they dragged Swammerdam's tortured soul down into dust and ruin.

The fates smiled on him only once, and ambiguously at that. The Prince of Tuscany proposed 12,000 florins for his collection of insects on condition that Swammerdam come and live in Florence—a tempting proposition—and that he accept Catholicism. This last condition was unacceptable for a man tortured by conflicts of conscience. He rejected the magnanimous offer.

A few years before his death (he died at the age of forty-three) he looked like a decrepit old man. Swammerdam's weak body resisted for a strangely long time, as if death despised its miserable prey and sentenced him to a long agony.

He experienced then that the world he had studied descended inside him: it nestled there and ravaged him from within. Long trains of ants marched through the corridors of his veins, swarms of bees drank the bitter nectar of his heart, large gray and brown moths slept on his eyes. The soul that usually flies to infinity at the moment of death left Swammerdam's tortured body prematurely. It could not bear the rustle of the wing cases, nor the senseless buzzing that disturbs the pure music of the Universe.

PERPETUUM MOBILE

❑

CORNELIS DREBBEL was a famous inventor and scholar, but his colleagues treated him with reserve, reproaching him for lack of seriousness. It is a fact he was more inclined to spectacular demonstrations of his numerous abilities than to carry out systematic research. This is probably why no university ever offered him a chair. The royal courts, however, adored him.

In 1604 he appeared in England. Within a short time he won the sympathy of the higher spheres and the monarch himself; the material proof of this was an annual pension, paid from the royal purse, and an apartment in Eltham Palace. Drebbel then became what might be called a full-time manufacturer of unusual things and phenomena: a supplier of miracles, producer of bewilderment and vertigo.

According to contemporary accounts, two events in particular (among many) caused a real sensation and remained for a long time in human memory: a demonstration of the navigation of a submarine, constructed by the inventor, which traveled from Westminster to Greenwich without emerging from the waters of the Thames; and a great meteorological pageant in Westminster Hall in London before the king, court, and invited guests. At the pageant Drebbel's machine hurled out thunder and lightning; suddenly in the middle of summer it became so freezing that walls were covered with frost and those who were present shivered from cold; at the end a warm, heavy rain fell and everyone melted in delight. There was no end to the applause in honor of this man who, by the power of his genius, made nature's forces compliant to his will.

Drebbel's head was full of ideas both big and small, serious and ridiculous, intelligent and completely insane. He constructed a special ladder to help obese people mount a horse, he worked out a new system to drain marshy terrain, he built flying machines (malicious people called them falling machines), he made a small hammer to hit parasites on the head that was connected to tweezers which pulled the victim from the hair, he invented a sensational technological process for dyeing fabrics, also an effigy that could be set in the wind and emit frightening cries and moans. This is just a small number of the inventions of this man of unusual resourcefulness.

Who was he in fact, a charlatan or scholar? Because we cannot look inside his soul, which has resided for a long time in the other world, we must concentrate our attention on what he left on earth. Drebbel's library in particular, a true curiosity, provides valuable indications for those who want to study the nature of his intellect, fertile, with strokes of genius and undisciplined at the same time.

The very arrangement of the books makes one think that Drebbel read scholarly works together with treatises by alchemists. The writings of Bacon, Leonardo da Vinci, and Giordano Bruno stood side by side with Paracelsus, *The Seventh Veil of Isis*, *The Temple of Hiram*, and *The Amphitheater of Eternal Wisdom*. The weed of gnosis was rampant in the garden of the natural sciences. On the margins of dissertations in the field of mechanics, chemistry, and ballistic science Drebbel drew esoteric diagrams and wrote the sonorous names of the cabala: Binah, Geburah, and Kether, which mean Intelligence, Force, and the Crown of Knowledge.

Drebbel thought the world could not be explained in purely scientific categories, that sometimes the immutable laws of nature are not obligatory, making room for miracles and dazzling wonder. Probably this is why he built a perpetual-motion machine, improving it throughout his life (he realized his enterprise was hopeless from the physicist's point of view). One has to admit that on this path of madness he obtained certain results. His pendulums, windmills, spheres of light metal with weights hanging from them moved for a long time indeed, and when movement stopped the inventor pushed them with a finger, like a demiurge, awakening sleepy matter from a nap.

After centuries when my bones have crumbled—Drebbel thought—and even my name has dissolved in mist, someone will find my clock eternally striking. I don't count on human memory but on the memory of the universe. I want my existence to be proved like the existence of God, with an unmistakable and infallible proof: from movement, *ex motu.*

HOME

❑

ONE can say with slight but certainly not great exaggeration that before travel began, a map existed first. Just as originally the hazy and impersonal outline of a poem drifts in the air for a long time before someone dares bring it to earth, giving it a shape understandable to men. Thus maps, the music of sirens' songs and challenges for the daring, suggested to the Dutch a bold plan to navigate to China by a northern passage: a dark, narrow, icy corridor rather than the commonly used tropical route, full of murderous pirates and equally murderous competitors.

The matter must have been treated in full seriousness, because the Estates General established an award of 25,000 florins for whoever would successfully realize this intention bordering on madness. Two experienced men of the sea, Captain Jacob von Heemskerck and the pilot Willem Barents, set out with a crew and two ships on a great reconnaissance. It was May 1597. The green strip of land quickly disappeared from view, and after barely three weeks the sailors were surrounded by an inconceivable polar world. On June 5 one of the deck hands shouted that he saw a flock of huge white swans on the horizon. These were actually mountains of ice. The sailor's mistake indicates not so much poetic imagination as a poor knowledge of polar hell.

After many dramatic episodes, adversities of weather and fate, struggles with an ever more incomprehensible environment (these wonders increased gradually, allowing partial adaptation), less than four months after leaving Holland further navigation became impossible. The ships were imprisoned by autumn ice on the shore of Nova Zemlya. A decision was made to winter there. For this they needed a house.

By happy coincidence they found wood on the island, brought by ocean currents from Siberian forests. It was hard as rock, but they managed with this resistant material. The ship's carpenter died at the beginning of construction; the frozen earth did not want to accept his mortal remains, and his body was buried in a crevasse of ice. Time was running out—the days were shorter and shorter, the temperature fell in an appalling way. Those who worked on the construction complained that when they put nails in their mouth according to the carpenter's custom, they froze to their lips and had to be torn off with the skin.

On the third of November the last board was finally nailed to the roof. The happy sailors decorated their home with a branch formed out of snow.

So here was the house: a miniature of their homeland, a shelter from frost and the polar bears that hunted the Dutchmen. There was hardly a day they did not meet them eye-to-eye. Rifles, flintlocks, muskets, halberds, and fire were used but did not help much; the stubbornness and persistance of all these animals were almost human as they suddenly appeared like white, bloodthirsty phantoms, climbing the roof and trying to enter through the chimney. They sniffed and panted threateningly at the house's door.

The chronicler of the expedition rarely permits himself to express emotions except for pious sighs to the Creator. At one point in his report he adopts the emotional term "beast" for the bear, and uses it until the end. In the middle of a polar night the bears' siege came to an end and polar foxes appeared; the chronicler has a tender and warm term for them, "creatures." They obediently entered the traps that were set, provided meat (it tasted like rabbit) and fur. Once again it was shown that the mythical brotherhood of men with those on all fours contains a certain dose of hypocrisy.

On earth that was not destined for man in God's plans, on the cruel, dazzlingly white and blindingly black chessboard of fate, stood a house. A fire set in the fireplace gave more smoke than warmth. Icy wind played in cracks caulked with moss. Sick with scurvy and consumed with fever, the men lay on bunks that hung from the walls, snow burying the small house with its chimney. The polar night confused all measures of time and reality. At the end of January, the sailors succumbed to a collective hallucination just like that of wanderers in the desert who have visions of an oasis—they saw an unreal sun above the horizon. But the funereal darkness of polar night was still to last for a long time.

It would be a mistake to think the hibernation of the Dutch was a kind of passive resistance. On the contrary, the energy that sparked from them is cause for admiration. They were busy, bustling like good Frisian peasants on their barren holdings. They carried wood for the fire, nursed sick companions, repaired the house; some of them wrote about the peculiarities of the surrounding world. They hunted, intricately practiced culinary arts, read the Bible aloud, entered four to a barrel while the ship's barber poured hot water over them. He also cut their hair, which grew amazingly fast, as if the body wanted to cover itself with fur. They sewed clothes and shoes from the hides of the animals they caught, sang pious and indecent songs. They repaired a clock that constantly froze, a clock that was consolation that time is not an abyss or black mask of nothingness but can be divided into a human yesterday and a human tomorrow—into a day without light and a night without glimmer, seconds, hours, and weeks, into doubt that goes away and hope that is born.

He who struggles with the elements in a deadly contest, with an adversary a hundred times stronger, realizes he has a chance only if he concentrates all his attention, will, and cunning to counter the blows. It requires a special reduction of the entire personality, a degradation to animal impulses dictated by instinct. It is necessary to forget who one used to be. What counts is only the very moment of thunder, fire, storm, blizzard, and earthquake. Any human surplus, any superfluous thought, feeling, or gesture can bring catastrophe.

The handful of Dutch sailors exposed to the utmost ordeal transgressed these iron rules at least two times. They added a human accent to the laws of struggle with impersonal nature. But perhaps it was not just a risky extravagance or sentimental song about attachment sung in the icy wilderness, but an important element of self-defense. Both events are related to their new home. Because—after all—it was a home.

On January 6, 1598, the day of Epiphany, without paying any attention to what was happening outside, the shipwrecked men decided to celebrate the holiday as in their homeland. Even sober Captain Heemskerck gave in to the madness, ordering a sizable portion of wine and two pounds of flour to be measured out to the crew from diminishing supplies; with this they baked a plum cake and biscuits. The mulled wine with spices put the crew in such high spirits that they started to dance; many times they went through their favorite "bungler," a hat dance, and a reel. They arranged a contest to decide who would become the Emperor of Nova Zemlya, and selected an Almond King. He was a very young sick sailor, Jacob Schiedamm, who died soon afterward, but on that memorable evening he smiled for the last time, to his companions rather than the world. The chronicler says everything took place as it did with their dear ones in Holland, which he summons only once with the solemn incantation "patria."

It is not known who first had the idea—it might have been a product of collective imagination—but when the house was finally built (to tell the truth, it was a doghouse) they decided to give it some style. A triangular portal was painted in black over the low door, and two windows were placed symmetrically on the front wall (the house was without windows). An eave made from shipboards was arranged in tiers and nailed to a flat roof. Soon it was swept away by a snowstorm, clearly hostile to these aesthetic subtleties.

When on June 13, 1598, they started back on two wretched boats, no one had the courage to look back at the deserted home—that monument to fidelity with a triangular portal and two false windows where pitchy darkness lurked.

SPINOZA'S BED

❏

It is an amazing thing that our memory best retains images of great philosophers when their lives were coming to an end. Socrates raising the chalice with hemlock to his mouth, Seneca whose veins were opened by a slave (there is a painting of this by Rubens), Descartes roaming cold palace rooms with a foreboding that his role of teacher of the Swedish queen would be his last, old Kant smelling a grated horseradish before his daily walk (the cane preceding him, sinking deeper and deeper into the sand), Spinoza consumed by tuberculosis and patiently polishing lenses, so weak he is unable to finish his *Treatise on the Rainbow* . . . A gallery of noble moribunds, pale masks, plaster casts.

In the eyes of his biographer, Spinoza was unmistakably an ideal wise man: exclusively concentrated on the precise architecture of his works, perfectly indifferent to material affairs, and liberated from all passions. But an episode in his life is passed over in silence by some biographers, while others consider it only an incomprehensible, youthful whim.

Spinoza's father died in 1656. In his family Baruch had the reputation of an eccentric young man who had no practical sense and wasted precious time studying incomprehensible books. Due to clever intrigues (his stepsister, Rebecca, and her husband, Casseres, played the main role) he was deprived of his inheritance. She hoped the absentminded young man would not even notice. But it happened otherwise.

144

Baruch initiated a lawsuit in court with an energy no one suspected him to have. He hired lawyers, called witnesses, was both matter-of-fact and passionate, extremely well-oriented in the most subtle details of procedure and convincing as a son injured and stripped of his rights.

They settled the division of the estate relatively quickly; clear legal rules existed in this matter. But then a second act of the trial unexpectedly followed, causing a general sense of unpleasantness and embarrassment.

As if the devil of possessiveness had entered him, Baruch began to litigate over almost each object from his father's house. It started with the bed in which his mother, Deborah, had died (he did not forget about its dark-green curtains). Then he requested objects without any value, explaining that he had an emotional attachment to them. The judges were monumentally bored, and could not understand where this irresistible desire in the ascetic young man came from. Why did he wish to inherit a poker, a pewter pot with a broken handle, an ordinary kitchen stool, a china figure representing a shepherd without a head, a broken clock that stood in the vestibule and was a home for mice, or a painting over the fireplace so completely blackened it looked like a self-portrait of tar?

Baruch won the trial. He could now sit with pride on his pyramid of spoils, casting spiteful glances at those who tried to disinherit him. But he did not do this. He only chose his mother's bed (with the dark-green curtains), giving the rest away to his adversaries defeated at the trial.

No one understood why he acted this way. It seemed an obvious extravagance, but in fact had a deeper meaning. It was as if Baruch wanted to say that virtue is not at all an asylum for the weak. The art of renunciation is an act of courage—it requires the sacrifice of things universally desired (not without hesitation and regret) for matters that are great and incomprehensible.

LETTER

❑

IT was accidentally discovered in the 1920s—to be exact, in 1924—in an antique-book shop in Leyden. Three sheets of cream-colored paper of the dimensions 11.5 by 17 centimeters, with traces of humidity, but the handwriting well preserved, the small, clear letters completely readable. An unknown person had pasted the letter onto the inside of the cover of an old, once very popular romance called *The Knight with a Swan,* published in 1651 by the Amsterdam firm of Cool.

The majority of scholars have written skeptically about this discovery—for example, Isarlo, Gillet, Clark, de Vries, Borrero, and Goldschneider; only a young poet and historian from Utrecht, van der Velde (later stabbed with a dagger in mysterious circumstances not far from Scheveningen), fiercely defended the authenticity of the letter to the end of his life. According to the young scholar, its author was none other than Johannes Vermeer, and its recipient Antony van Leeuwenhoek, a naturalist whose merits in the field of improving the microscope are well known. The scholar and the artist were both born in the same year, the same day, and spent their entire lives in the same city.

The letter shows no traces of corrections or subsequent interpolations, but it contains two spelling mistakes and changes; obviously it must have been written in a hurry. A few lines have been crossed out so decidedly and energetically that we will never learn what foolish or shameful thoughts were covered forever by the blackness of the ink.

The handwriting with its pointed letters, "v" written like an open eight, a somewhat wavy movement of the pen as if someone was speeding up and then suddenly stopping, reveals a striking similarity if not identity with the only preserved signature of Vermeer in the register of Saint Luke's Guild in 1662. Chemical analysis of the paper and ink allows us to date the document at the second half of the seventeenth century. Everything indicates, then, that the letter could have been written by Vermeer's hand, yet we lack irrefutable proofs. We know that technically perfect falsifications have been made.

All those who spoke against the authenticity of the document put forward numerous arguments, but to tell the truth, they are not too convincing. Scholarly prudence and even far-reaching skepticism are undoubtedly praiseworthy virtues. But one could sense something between the lines of the critical remarks that no one clearly stated: the main reservations were caused by the letter's content. Let us suppose that if Vermeer wrote to his mother-in-law, Maria Tins, asking her to lend him a hundred florins for the baptism of his son, Ignatius, or let us also imagine if he offered one of his paintings to his baker van Buyten as a guarantee against a debt, I believe no one would protest. But when after two and a half centuries the Great Mute speaks with his own voice, and what he says is an intimate confession—a manifesto and a prophecy—we don't want to accept it because we have a great fear before a revelation, and withhold of consent to a miracle.

Here is the letter:

Undoubtedly You will be surprised I am writing rather than simply dropping by your laboratory before dusk, as so often happens. But I think I do not have enough courage, I do not know how to tell you to your face what you will read in a moment.

147

I would prefer not to write this letter. I hesitated for a long time, because I really did not want to expose our long friendship to danger. Finally I made up my mind to do it. There are, after all, things more important than what unites us, more important than Leeuwenhoek, more important than Vermeer.

A few days ago you showed me a drop of water under your new microscope. I always thought it was pure like glass, while in reality strange creatures swirl in it like in Bosch's transparent hell. During this demonstration you watched my consternation intently, and I think with satisfaction. Between us there was silence. Then you said very slowly and deliberately: "Such is water, my dear, such and not otherwise."

I understood what you wanted to say: that we artists record appearances, the life of shadows and the deceptive surface of the world; we do not have the courage or ability to reach the essence of things. We are craftsmen, so to speak, who work in the matter of illusion, while you and those like you are the masters of truth.

As you know my father owned the tavern Mechelen at the marketplace. An old sailor often came there who had wandered all over the world, from Indochina to Brazil and from Madagascar to the Arctic Ocean. I remember him well. He was always quite tipsy but told splendid stories, and everyone gladly listened to him. He was the attraction of the place, like a big colorful picture or exotic animal. One of his favorite stories was about the Chinese emperor Shi Huang-ti.

This emperor ordered his country to be surrounded by a thick wall, in order to shut out everything that was different. He burned all books so he would not have to listen to the admonishing voice of the past; he forbade cultivation of any of the arts under penalty of death. (Their complete uselessness was blatantly clear when they were compared to such important tasks of state as building a fortress, or cutting off rebels' heads.) Thus poets, painters, and musicians hid in the mountains and remote monasteries; they led the life of exiles tracked by a pack of informers. On the squares piles of paintings were burned, fans, statues, ornate fabrics, objects of luxury, and all things that

148

could be considered pretty. Men, women, and children all wore the same ash-colored clothes. The emperor declared war even on flowers; he ordered their fields to be buried under stones. A special decree announced that at sunset everyone was to be at home, the windows tightly covered with black curtains because (you know yourself) what incredible pictures can be painted by the wind, clouds, and the light of sunset.

The emperor valued only science. He showered scientists with honors and gold. Every day astronomers would bring news of the discovery of a new or imaginary star. In servile fashion it was given the name of the emperor, and soon the entire firmament teemed with the luminous points of Shi Huang-ti I, Shi Huang-ti II, Shi Huang-ti III, and so on. Mathematicians labored to invent new numerical systems, complicated equations, and unimaginable geometrical figures, knowing only too well their labors were sterile, of no use to anyone. Naturalists promised they would develop a tree whose crown was embedded in the ground and whose roots reached the sky, also a wheat grain as large as a fist.

At last the emperor wished for immortality. Physicians performed cruel experiments on men and animals to discover the secret of the eternal heart, the eternal liver, eternal lungs.

As it often happens with men of action, the emperor desired to change the face of the earth and sky so his name would be inscribed forever in the memory of future generations. He did not understand that the life of an ordinary peasant, shoemaker, or grocer was far more worthy of respect and admiration, while he himself was becoming a bloodless letter, a symbol among countless symbols of madness and violence monotonously repeating themselves.

After all the crimes, all the devastation he caused in human minds and souls, his own death was cruelly banal: he choked on a single grape. To remove him from the surface of the earth, nature did not exert herself to produce a hurricane or deluge.

Probably you will ask: Why do I tell you all this, and what is the connection between the story of the foreign ruler and your drop of water? I will most likely answer you not very clearly or coherently, hoping you will understand the words of a man who is full of forebodings and anxiety.

I am afraid that you and others like you are setting out on a dangerous journey that might bring humanity not only advantages but also great, irreparable harm. Haven't you noticed that the more the means and tools of observation are perfected, the more distant and elusive become the goals? With each new discovery a new abyss opens. We are more and more lonely in the mysterious void of the universe.

I know that you want to lead men out of the labyrinths of superstition and chance, that you want to give them certain, clear knowledge, which according to you is the only defense against fear and anxiety. But will it really bring us relief if we substitute the word *necessity* for the word *Providence*?

Most likely you will reproach me that our art does not solve any of the enigmas of nature. Our task is not to solve enigmas, but to be aware of them, to bow our heads before them and also to prepare the eyes for never-ending delight and wonder. If you absolutely require discoveries, however, I will tell you that I am proud to have succeeded in combining a certain particularly intensive cobalt with a luminous, lemonlike yellow, as well as recording the reflection of southern light that strikes through thick glass onto a gray wall.

The tools we use are indeed primitive: a stick with a bunch of bristles attached to the end, a rectangular board, pigments and oils. These have not changed for centuries, like the human body and nature. If I understand my task, it is to reconcile man with surrounding reality. This is why I and my guild brothers repeat an infinite number of times the sky and clouds, the portraits of men and cities, all these odds and ends of the cosmos, because only there do we feel safe and happy.

Our paths part. I know I will not convince you, and that you will not abandon polishing lenses or erecting your Tower of Babel. But allow us as well to continue our archaic procedure, to tell the world words of reconciliation and to speak of joy from recovered harmony, of the eternal desire for reciprocated love.

EPILOGUE

❑

CORNELIS TROOST, textile merchant and unknown hero of history, is dying.

It is not true our entire life appears in front of our eyes before death. That great recapitulation of existence is an invention of the poets. In fact we sink into chaos. Within Cornelis Troost there is a confusion of days and nights, he does not distinguish Monday from Sunday, he confuses three in the afternoon with four in the morning; when he is alert he waits, listening to his own breathing and his heart. He asks for a clock to be put on a table in front of his bed, as if hoping he will experience the grace of cosmic order. But what is nine o'clock if it does not mean sitting at the desk in the office, the noon hour without the stock exchange, four o'clock from which dinner is taken away, six o'clock without coffee and a pipe, eight o'clock deprived of all meaning because they have removed the table, supper, family, and friends. O holy ritual of everydayness, without you time is empty like a falsified inventory that corresponds to no real objects.

The angels of death keep vigil at his bed. Soon the naked soul of Cornelis Troost will stand before the Highest Judge to account for his deeds. We who know little about divine matters are interested in a human, unimportant question: Was he happy?

Friendly fate led him by the hand that memorable April day when half a century earlier he wandered through huge, noisy Amsterdam, clutching a letter that recommended him to a relative who was a shoemaker. It contained a request to kindly accept the boy and teach him the profession. That letter, conceived by a teacher in the country, had only one drawback: there was no address.

Then, as it happens only in fairy tales, a handsome man dressed in black appeared before the lost boy: Baltazar Jong, a textile merchant who without asking many questions took him to his house, gave him a bed in the attic, and entrusted him with the responsible function of message boy. Thus without effort or merits Cornelis passed from the purgatory of twine and lasts—which seemed to be his destiny—to the heaven of silks and laces. Such was the beginning of a stunning career, as it is only a natural course of events and not a career when the son of a mayor becomes mayor and the son of an admiral becomes an admiral.

Cornelis Troost commendably passed all the steps of the merchants' profession. He was a conscientious and zealous apprentice, scribe, warehouseman, accountant, salesman favored by the ladies because of his constantly pink cheeks, finally a kind of personal secretary of Jong. Then he changed his quarters from the attic, which meant he was now treated as a member of the family, not numerous but honest and consisting of the master, the lady of the house, and a daughter.

At about this time he performed an unusual deed: carrying an important, confidential message, he skated the distance from Amsterdam to Leyden in less than an hour along frozen canals. (Ungrateful human memory has not recorded this fact as it deserved.) Mr. Jong took care to put a healthy soul in the healthy body of his pupil. He sent him to dancing lessons, taught him the flute and a few Latin proverbs. The one Cornelis liked most was *Hic Rhodus, hic salta,* and he would insert it in his conversations with important persons only too often, sometimes even without much sense.

Mr. Jong was a man of broad horizons, educated and subtle. He had collected a sizable library. The classics stood in the first rows, while shamefully hidden behind them were passionate accounts of faraway voyages that were to push his grandson to the stormy life of an adventurer. He bought paintings, and was interested in astronomy. In the evening he strummed a guitar and read Latin poets; he preferred, however, his native Vondel. He systematically enlarged his collection of minerals. Above all he adored Livy, oysters, Italian opera, and light Rhine wines. His sudden death plunged his family and friends in genuine sadness. He died as stylishly as he lived—at a full table, as he was lifting a sponge cake dipped in wine to his mouth.

Without waiting for tears to dry, Cornelis Troost asked for the hand of the daughter of his deceased master, Anna. He was not moved by a mercenary motive, at least he did not think so, although at the same time he realized he had entered his adopted family not by the front door but by the attic. At this moment he felt as noble as Perseus, who frees Andromeda chained to the rock of an orphan's mourning.

His proposal was accepted (who could better lead the business of the firm?) and the wedding was arranged quickly (the malicious said too quickly). It was not too ostentatious, as circumstances did not allow it, but the tables bent under the food and beverages. Because of an excessive number of toasts washed down with wine, grain spirits, rum, and beer, Cornelis spent the wedding night in a state of complete unconsciousness.

A year after the wedding an only son was born, given the name of Jan at baptism.

The firm (it carried now the name "Jong, Troost and Son") was doing excellent business, thanks not only to favorable conditions but above all to Troost's talents and his unusual merchant's intuition. Born a peasant, he knew his countrymen were conservative to the marrow of their bones. One would think the owner of a large textile store would be interested in fashion. Troost simply ignored it, considering it a nuisance, like a runny nose that from time to time bothers an organism full of healthy habits and tastes. If he paid attention to the "latest rages" of fashion, it was only in the domain of accessories: ribbons, shoulder straps, buckles, and eventually feathers. He firmly believed that true elegance does not demand a broken line or richness of colors but is satisfied with the calm, simple line of a cut, as well as noble black, purple, and white. He was also, if one may say so, an ardent patriot of native industry. He was convinced—and persuaded his clients—that the best wool comes from Leyden, the cotton from Haarlem has no competition, Amsterdam's silk fabrics are truly without equal, and there are no better velvets on earth than those from Utrecht.

Cornelis Troost, owner of the firm "Jong, Troost and Son," worked untiringly six days a week, but he devoted Sundays and holidays entirely to his family. From early spring until late fall, after hearing a service the Troosts would set out on faraway excursions to the Three Oaks, the dunes, or to an inn, Da Zwaan, situated in a picturesque and secluded spot. Here is a picture: Cornelis marches in front (always some hundred feet ahead, as if bursting with the memory of his old skating exploits), silent Anna is walking with small steps behind him. The servant with a basket of monstrous dimensions full of victuals, and small noisy Jan, riding a cart harnessed to a goat, close the procession. Both parents spoiled their only child beyond all imagination. A rest. Lunch in the shade of old elms: cream, wild strawberries, cherries, rye bread, butter, cheese, wine, and cake.

In the early afternoon the family would come to the inn Da

Zwaan, famous for its excellent cuisine and situated near a major road crossing. Gallows stood there; one could tactfully go around them by choosing a path through the meadows. Inside the inn it was always crowded and noisy. Heavy odors of tobacco, lamb fat, and beer wafted in the air. Cornelis Troost usually ordered *hutsepot*—one could not find a better one in all the United Provinces—a salmon in green sauce, incomparable crepes, and candied chestnuts (he would put them thoughtfully in his pocket, fearing a sudden attack of hunger on the way back). Washed down with a double beer from Delft, all this put body and soul in a state of satiated melancholy.

The return would take place slowly, in reverse order: Jan rode in front, next to him the servant freed from her burden, behind them Anna fearfully looking back, and at the end Cornelis, who would frequently stop. As if suddenly struck by the beauty of existence and the loveliness of nature, he craned his neck and greeted the passing clouds with loud singing not completely concordant with principles of harmony:

> Good evening, good evening,
> my dear Joosje

or:

> Lush oaklands, lovely crags
> Noble witnesses of my pleasures

If now or several years later Cornelis Troost was asked whether he was happy, he would not have known what to answer. Happy people, just as people who are healthy, do not ponder about their own condition.

O wonderful clock measuring weekdays and holidays! It is true that Cornelis Troost never stood in the blinding glare of great historical events. But could one say that in the drama of the world he played a secondary role? He met his fate of tex-

155

tile merchant as others meet their roles of warriors, heretics, or statesmen. He rubbed against history only once, fleetingly, as in a dance—it happened during the visit of a foreign monarch.

At that time Troost was an elder of the guild, and he went to the town hall for the welcoming ceremony wearing an orange sash, yellow ribbons below his knees and at his shoulders. He wore a fanciful hat decorated with black ostrich feathers that with every breath of wind almost took flight. From the depths of his heart he hated these clothes, pompous as costumes of opera singers, but he did not regret this masquerade, because he saw the monarch face-to-face—that is, from a human perspective. Later he repeated an endless number of times: "I saw him quite close, and you know he is pale, fat, small, about half a head shorter than me." He was bursting with great republican pride.

After the reception there was a procession in honor of the monarch, combined with shooting into the innocent sky. For the second time Troost had an occasion to try out his beautiful Florentine rifle. The first time it happened in his own garden when he fired at an owl suspected of disturbing the peace at night. The stock of the rifle was decorated with an engraving of "The Judgment of Paris" against a background of a vast mountainous landscape. Cornelis valued this part of the weapon most, considering the metal pipe a superfluous addition.

After these historical events life continued to roll in its ordinary groove. Business went splendidly, but Jan gave his parents constant troubles and worries: he did not study, ran away from home, and preferred the company of total scoundrels. The prodigal son always returned to the bosom of the family, however, where a biblical scene took place, full of tears, repentance, and forgiveness. It seemed that in the end matters would settle down favorably for everyone. Only, Anna was getting weak, and so it was decided to accept a third servant; among many candidates a young Frisian peasant by the name of Judith was selected.

Her beauty was not dazzling, but it awoke in the soul of the master of the house hazy, sweet memories of distant childhood. He liked her very much, and gave her ribbons and barrettes matching her red, fluffy hair, asking her not to tell anyone about it. He persuaded his wife to permit Judith to help him in the store in the evening. It might have happened two or three times that they stayed alone and locked the door with a key. But the bad tongues of the neighbors gossiped about the scandal. Anna suffered ostentatiously but in silence.

Cornelis started to go more often to the barber. He played the flute for hours. He became talkative, loud, and excessively gay. One day he confided to Anna that he wanted to order a portrait. A painter was recommended who lived on Rozengracht. He was, or else had been, a fashionable portrait painter and was also known for his religious scenes. Festively dressed, Cornelis went to him: the name escaped his memory, but passersby showed him the house. The painter received him not too politely. He had closely set, piercing eyes, and the thick hands of a butcher. He was dressed in a long, stained apron and had a strange turban on his head. All of this would have been bearable, but the price for the portrait that this boor gave him—300 florins—confused Cornelis (he immediately calculated it against yards of good woolen fabric). An embarrassing silence followed. At last the painter declared that he could portray Cornelis as a Pharisee, and then the price would be considerably lower. At this point it was the hurt pride of the textile merchant that took over. He wanted to be represented as he was, at the peak of success, in a gentle glow of happiness but without unnecessary symbols and decorations, with his own large head surrounded by luxuriant hair, his keen eyes looking into the future with confidence, a thick nose, the mouth of a gourmet, and also strong hands, resting near the frame of the painting, in which one could entrust not only the business matters of the firm "Jong, Troost and Son" but also the fate of the city (at the time, Cornelis dreamt of being mayor). It is not surprising that the contract for the painting was never signed. Later, someone gave him the name of another famous portrait painter from Haarlem; but he did not contact him, because his mind was preoccupied with serious problems and worries.

One never knows when or from where a storm will come that shakes the foundations of a house (and it seemed to be eternal), and in the sudden flash of lightning show the emptiness of plans arduously put together during an entire life. Jan, the only son, the hope and future heir of the firm, ran away from home for good. He left a letter that he had found a job on a ship, and even gave its name. But they quickly discovered there was no such ship. Thus, only the grim supposition remained that the boy—in fact, already a man—had joined the pirates, those scoundrels who throw the Bible, rosary, and logbook overboard and finish a life of crime in dungeons or on the gallows.

For the first time Troost felt wronged, helpless, and humiliated. Anna suffered also, but quietly, in the depths of her impenetrable maternal being. On the other hand, the extensive suffering of Cornelis encompassed many different spheres of his soul: he was frightened by the unexpected blow of fortune that had been well-disposed until now but suddenly revealed its true, sneering face. He felt stripped of his good name and merits. A cruel sentence constantly returned in his thoughts: "I am now just a father of a criminal." He lost faith in the only human immortality expressed in the hope that the name Troost—surrounded by human respect and trust—would be repeated forever in the guild of textile merchants.

What is more, the affair with Judith (according to Cornelis, there was no affair) was becoming more and more notorious. Indeed, after closing the shop he stayed longer and longer with her, ample cause for gossip. Acquaintances answered his greetings with a wink and an impish smile that probably meant, "Well well, we did not know you were such a brave boy." On the other hand, during church service his neighbors in the pew preferred to stand on the stone floor, to let him know the void surrounding him expressed severe rebuke. For the good of the firm, therefore, he decided to let the girl go. He accompanied her to the square from which carriages left in the direction of Hoorn; he hugged her in a fatherly way, pressing into her hand fourteen florins and eight stoovers.

She disappeared in the crowd. He did not know whether she entered the carriage. If she went to the tavern on the other side of the street, At the Black Cock, which had the worst reputation (sailors hungry for cheap love knew it well), her fate was sealed. This thought, and especially the lustful images associated with her, haunted him for years.

He worked with his old energy, but without the enthusiasm that gives wings to all enterprises. Sometimes he refused to buy large shipments of merchandise even on advantageous terms, saying: "I leave it to the young; now I make the rounds of my estate and check walls, locks, and chains." The business, however, went no worse than before.

In the spring, Anna died.

Now he was alone. He thought for some time that he should crown the memory of himself and Anna with stone. It was to be a bas-relief built into the wall of Nieuw Kerk representing the couple holding each other's hands, with a quotation from the Bible underneath: "Thus I repent and do penance in dust and ashes." But the common sense of Cornelis, which never abandoned him even when he approached spheres not subject to reason (rarely, it is true), suggested that he who truly humbles himself before the Lord does not erect marble monuments to himself. He pushed the temptation aside. "A simple plaque on the floor of the church will be enough," he said, surprised at his own modesty.

A new idea liberated unsuspected reserves of initiative, inventiveness, and enthusiasm. He managed to convince his exceedingly economical guild brothers (for years he had been dean of the guild) that it was necessary to build an orphanage. The spirit of a young entrepreneur entered Cornelis, more, an apostle of a cause. He tried to be everywhere at once: he organized collections, banquets, and lotteries to add to the funds of the enterprise, he approved plans, supervised the progress of construction, conferred for hours with masons and carpenters about every detail. He liked to stroll in the courtyard of the future orphanage and draw with his cane against the sky the still nonexistent walls and windows, floors, moldings, and steep roof.

He spent evenings at home "in the yellow room" whose windows gave onto the garden. An armchair upholstered with red cordovan stood there in which Mr. Jong (how many years ago it was) read his Latin poets half aloud. It was the most venerable piece of furniture in the household, like a flagship commanding a flotilla of beds, tables, benches, chairs, abysmal wardrobes, and cupboards. Cornelis would take a few books from the library at random and sink into that armchair, leafing through the last number of the *Dutch Mercury,* in which there was always so much interesting news about floods, court intrigues, the exchange, miracles, and crimes. He did not read much; he listened to the hubbub of the street and murmurs in the house. A strong smell came from the garden of narcissus, wild roses, and saffron.

As he let himself be carried away by sounds and smells, he had the experience that time was no longer docile. Before, during his youth, he was its master; he knew how to stop or accelerate it like a fisherman who imposes his own rhythm on the current of a river. Now he felt like a stone thrown to the bottom, a stone covered with moss over which a mobile immensity of incomprehensible waters was rolling.

The book would slip off his knees. He fell into torpor. More and more often the servant had to wake him for supper.

Soon after his birthday, which was celebrated with pomp (he had turned sixty), he fell sick. The doctors diagnosed a jaundiced fever, recommended peace, and gave assurances that the patient would quickly return to health. Cautious Cornelis made a testament and ordered that debts be paid back ahead of time. The state of the firm was as follows: assets, 12,000 florins; liabilities easy to collect, 9,300 florins; 5,100 florins in valuable papers and shares in the East India Company.

He was getting weaker and weaker; now he no longer got up from bed. The physicians prescribed herb compresses, different potions: quinine wine, tincture of aloes, extract of gentian. They also let his blood, and in the end recommended that spider heads in walnut shells be applied to the chest of the patient; if that did not help, verses from the Bible could be substituted for the spider heads. Clearly, science was discreetly giving way to faith.

Every day around five—it was a sunny, very warm summer—an old friend of Troost would come, Abraham Anslo, once a preacher famous throughout Holland, today a silent old man with a sparse gray beard and permanently tearing eyes. He sat at the foot of the bed. They smiled to each other, their dialogue taking place beyond words and time. The patient had a huge need to confess his doubts, spiritual perplexities, and anxieties. He could not understand the Other World at all. The empty blue skies frightened him. Very likely it was an impious rebellion of the imagination, above all of the pagan senses. He was absolutely unable to understand how one can exist without a house, without creaking stairs and a banister, without curtains and candelabra, also without the cloth that had surrounded him throughout his life. What implacable force takes away from us the coolness of coarse silk, black wool flowing through the hands like a gentle wave, linen recalling the surface of a pond covered with ice, velvet tickling like moss, laces that seemed to whisper women's secrets?

Anslo would leave before dusk, and touch the hand of his friend with cold fingers for good-bye.

Not much time remained.

Tomorrow, the day after tomorrow a servant would enter with breakfast and give a short cry.

Then they would cover all the mirrors in the house, and turn all the pictures to the walls so the image of a girl writing a letter, of ships in open sea, of peasants dancing under a tall oak, would not stop the one who wanders toward unimaginable worlds from going on his way.